To the Reader

This book is presented in its original form and is part of the religious literature and works of Scientology® Founder, L. Ron Hubbard. It is a record of Mr. Hubbard's observations and research into the nature of man and each individual's capabilities as a spiritual being, and is not a statement of claims made by the author, publisher or any Church of Scientology.

Scientology is defined as the study and handling of the spirit in relationship to itself, universes and other life. Thus, the mission of the Church of Scientology is a simple one: to help the individual regain his true nature, as a spiritual being, and thereby attain an awareness of his relationship with his fellow man and the universe. Therein lies the path to personal integrity, trust, enlightenment, and spiritual freedom itself.

Scientology and its forerunner and substudy, Dianetics, as practiced by the Church, address only the "thetan" (spirit), which is senior to the body, and its relationship to and effects on the body. While the Church is free, as all churches are, to engage in spiritual healing, its primary goal is increased spiritual awareness for all. For this reason, neither Scientology nor Dianetics is offered as, nor professes to be physical healing, nor is any claim made to that effect. The Church does not accept individuals who desire treatment of physical or mental illness but, instead, requires a competent medical examination for physical conditions, by qualified specialists, before addressing their spiritual cause.

The Hubbard® Electrometer, or E-Meter, is a religious artifact used in the Church. The E-Meter, by itself, does nothing and is only used by ministers and ministers-in-training, qualified in its use, to help parishioners locate the source of spiritual travail.

The attainment of the benefits and goals of the Scientology religion requires each individual's dedicated participation, as only through one's own efforts can they be achieved.

We hope reading this book is only one step of a personal voyage of discovery into this new and vital world religion.

THIS BOOK BELONGS TO

Kerry Noonan

SCIENTOLOGY
THE FUNDAMENTALS
OF THOUGHT

SCIENTOLOGY
THE FUNDAMENTALS OF THOUGHT

L. RON HUBBARD

Bridge
Publications, Inc.

A
HUBBARD®
PUBLICATION

Bridge Publications, Inc.
5600 E. Olympic Boulevard
Commerce, California 90022

ISBN 978-1-4031-4420-1

Printed in the United States of America

IMPORTANT NOTE

In reading this book, be very certain you never go past a word you do not fully understand. The only reason a person gives up a study or becomes confused or unable to learn is because he or she has gone past a word that was not understood.

The confusion or inability to grasp or learn comes AFTER a word the person did not have defined and understood. It may not only be the new and unusual words you have to look up. Some commonly used words can often be misdefined and so cause confusion.

This datum about not going past an undefined word is the most important fact in the whole subject of study. Every subject you have taken up and abandoned had its words which you failed to get defined.

Therefore, in studying this book be very, very certain you never go past a word you do not fully understand. If the material becomes confusing or you can't seem to grasp it, there will be a word just earlier that you have not understood. Don't go any further, but go back to BEFORE you got into trouble, find the misunderstood word and get it defined.

GLOSSARY

To aid reader comprehension, L. Ron Hubbard directed the editors to provide a glossary. This is included in the Appendix, *Editor's Glossary of Words, Terms and Phrases*. Words sometimes have several meanings. The *Editor's Glossary* only contains the definitions of words as they are used in this text. Other definitions can be found in standard language or Dianetics and Scientology dictionaries.

If you find any other words you do not know, look them up in a good dictionary.

$\mathcal{F}$OREWORD

 HIS THIN BOOK is a summation, if brief, of the results of fifty thousand years of thinking men. Their materials, researched and capped by a quarter of a century of original search by L. Ron Hubbard, have brought the humanities, so long outdistanced by the "exact sciences," into a state of equality, if not superiority, to physics, chemistry and mathematics.

Mr. Hubbard, an American, studied nuclear physics at George Washington University in Washington, DC, before he started his studies about the mind, spirit and life. This explains the mathematical precision of the Scientology religion.

What has been attempted by a thousand universities and foundations, at a cost of billions, has been completed quietly here.

This *is* how life works. This *is* how you change men and women and children for the better.

The use or neglect of this material may well determine the use or neglect of the atomic bomb by Man. Scientology is already winning in this field. In the same period in history, two of the most sweeping forces Man has known have come to fruition: A knowledge of himself and others with Scientology; a means of destroying himself and all others by atomic fission. Which force wins depends in a large measure on your use of Scientology.

Equipped with this book alone, the student of Scientology can begin a practice and perform seeming miracles in changing the states of well-being, ability and intelligence of people.

No such knowledge has ever before existed, and no such results have ever before been attainable by Man, as those which can be reached by a study of this brief volume.

Give this book to a man or a woman in trouble, a man or a woman with an inquiring nature, a man or a woman with associates who need a better life, and let that man or woman study this volume carefully and apply it. Change and a better life will result.

Scientology is today around the world, represented on every continent on Earth with hundreds of millions of books in circulation.

We trust you will find this volume of use and hope that by placing it in your hands, you and many others can lead better lives.

NOTE ON
TRANSLATIONS:

*The
text of this book was
organized so that a complete
translation of all of it would deliver, without
interruption or destructive change, the basics of
Scientology into every language. The difficulties of
translation were most apparent when one was asked to
translate Scientology who had not had years of experience
with it. A translation not based on experience would
then be colored by the various misunderstandings of
the translator and when the work passed, translated,
into the hands of someone for use or study in that
tongue, the person was deprived of much of the
precision of Scientology. Thus, in order to secure
exact meanings, all words and some phrases
of questionable status in translation
were given in synonym.*

CONTENTS

PART ONE: *Basic Principles*

PART TWO: *Scientology Processing*

PREFACE

CIENTOLOGY AND SCIENTOLOGISTS are not revolutionaries. They are evolutionaries. They do not stand for overthrow. They stand for the improvement of what we have.

Scientology is not political. When the fires of ideology threaten to consume us all, it is time to forget politics and seek reason.

The mission of Scientology is not conquest — it is civilization. It is a war upon stupidity, the stupidity which leads us toward the Last War of All.

To a Scientologist, the real barbarism of Earth is *stupidity*. Only in the black muck of ignorance can the irrational conflicts of ideologies germinate.

Government, to a Scientologist, is a thing of reason and all problems of government can be resolved by reason.

Perhaps in yesterday one could afford the exploitation of ignorance for the sake of fancied gain. Perhaps in yesterday the study of the mind and reason was something for a summer afternoon. Perhaps in that same yesterday one amongst us could afford his irresponsibility and hate.

But that was yesterday. Today, exploited ignorance, a dilettante attitude toward existing knowledge, a refusal to assume one's role as a responsible member of the human race may be punished in the searing thunderclap of H-bombs released by men whose intelligence and statecraft were incapable of a better solution. Ignorant people elect ignorant rulers. And only ignorant rulers lead to war—and this time will lead to a war which will bring silence forever after to Earth.

As your associates, their homes, their children, their possessions and all their future lie ending in a radioactive street, there won't be time for us to wish we'd worked harder, been less easily dissuaded from pressing our arguments. The copies of this book you did *not* distribute will lie there too.

Some say they have no fear of death until the midnight of their dying is at hand. They say different then.

Those who strike at this work out of some black well of ideological misorientation, some antisocial cravenness, strike at the heart of Man—for Man has been a long time on the track to reason and Scientology can take him there.

There is not much Earth time. We must work.

The criminal is ignorant and stupid. Ignorance and stupidity may therefore be called criminal.

Cause Man to lay aside his hates and listen. Freedom from ignorance is at hand. Perhaps *that* was the Kingdom of Heaven.

There is not much Earth time in which to distribute this knowledge.

This is *the* solution to our barbarism out of which we would lose all.

Scientology works. *We* must work, all of us — not to harangue Man toward impossible freedoms, but to make Man civilized enough to be worthy of his freedom.

It is time Man grew up. That is what we have in mind. For there can be but weeping in the night where ignorance, factionalism, hatred and exploitation are served by the most ferocious and final weapon of all — the H-bomb.

Change no man's religion, change no man's politics, interrupt the sovereignty of no nation. Instead, teach Man to use what he has and what he knows to the factual creation, within *any* political reference, of a civilization on Earth for the first time.

And so we work.

SCIENTOLOGY
QUESTIONS AND ANSWERS

What is Scientology?

CIENTOLOGY EMBRACES and treats of human ability.

The term Scientology is taken from the Latin word *scio* (knowing, in the fullest meaning of the word) and the Greek word *logos* (study of). Scientology is further defined as "the study and handling of the spirit in relationship to itself, universes and other life."

Dianetics is a forerunner and substudy of Scientology. Dianetics comes from the Greek words *dia* (through) and *nous* (mind or soul). Dianetics is "what the soul is doing to the body."

Neither Dianetics nor Scientology should be confused with "modern" psychology. More acceptable and normal psychology, such as that begun by Saint Thomas Aquinas and extended by many later authors, was (in 1879) interrupted severely by one Professor Wundt, a Marxist at Leipzig University in Germany.

This man conceived that Man was an animal without soul and based all of his work on the principle that there was no *psyche* (a Greek word meaning "spirit"). Psychology, "the study of the spirit," then came into the peculiar position of being "a study of the spirit which *denied* the spirit." For the subsequent decades, Wundtian "psychology" was taught broadly throughout the world. It taught that Man was an animal. It taught that Man could not be bettered. It taught that intelligence never changed. This subject, Wundtian psychology, became standard mainly because of the indifference or lack of knowledge of people in charge of universities.

Scientology is actually a *new* but very basic psychology, in the most exact meaning of the word—"a study of the spirit." It can and does change behavior and intelligence and it can and does assist people to study life. Unlike Wundtian pseudo-psychology, it has no political aspiration. Scientology is not teaching dialectical materialism (the Marxist theory that all things are material, including the mind and spirit) under the heading of "psychology." As has been the tradition for thousands of years, the study of the spirit and all spiritual matters rightfully belong to religion.

Scientology, used by the trained and untrained person, can improve the health, intelligence, ability, behavior, skill and appearance of people.

The Scientology religion is precise and exact, designed for an age of exact sciences.

Scientology is employed by an *auditor* (a Scientology practitioner). The word auditor means "one who listens, a listener."

The auditor uses a set of *processes* (drills and exercises) upon individuals, or small and large groups of people, in their presence. The auditor makes these people, at their choice, do various exercises (processes) and these exercises bring about changes for the better in intelligence, behavior and general competence.

Scientology is employed, as well, by business and government persons to solve problems and to establish better organizations.

It is also employed by the average person to bring better order into life.

How is Scientology used?

Scientology is employed by an *auditor* (one who listens, a listener) as a set of drills (exercises, processes) upon the individual and small or large groups. It is also employed as an educational (teaching) subject.

It has been found that persons can be *processed* (drilled) in Scientology, with Scientology exercises, and can be made well of many, many psychosomatic illnesses (physical illnesses caused by the mind or spirit) and can become brighter, more alert and more competent. *But* if they are *only* processed, they have a tendency to be overwhelmed or startled. And although they may be brighter and more competent, they are still held down by an ignorance of life.

Therefore it is far better to teach *and* process (audit, drill) a person than only to process him. In other words, the best use of Scientology is through processing and education in Scientology. In this way there is no imbalance.

It is interesting that people only need to study Scientology to have some small rise in their own intelligence, behavior and competence. The study itself is therapeutic by actual testing.

Scientology is also used by business and government leaders to establish or improve organization.

It is used, as well, by the individual at home or at his work to make a better life.

Can a person use Scientology without much study?

Scientology is practiced in daily life by enormous numbers of people who have no formal training beyond a study of textbooks. Scientology was developed to be used by such people as well as by the trained practitioner. A person studying by himself from textbooks can use Scientology to help his fellow human beings.

Where is there more information about Scientology?

There are Churches of Scientology located on every continent throughout the world. Addresses can be found at the back of this book. Scientology practitioners are validated (certified and given certificates) by these organizations. Certificates are given only after very exact and precise training. A person who is skilled in Scientology has a certificate from one of these Church organizations. These offices and these people can give you more information about Scientology. They have many books on the subjects of Scientology and Dianetics and the various services offered by Churches of Scientology.

"A person studying by himself from textbooks can use Scientology to help his fellow human beings."

Part One

BASIC PRINCIPLES

BASIC PRINCIPLES

Chapter One

BASIC PRINCIPLES

 IKE ENGINEERING, Scientology has certain basic principles. These are necessary to a full understanding of the subject. It is not enough to know how to process (drill) people in Scientology. To be effective (good) one must also know the basic principles. Scientology is very exact. The humanities (human studies) of the past were full of opinions. Scientology is full of facts that work.

To study Scientology, one should scan quickly through the basics and find something with which one can agree. Having found *one thing* (one fact) with which he can agree, one should then skim through again and find another fact. One should continue to do this until he feels some friendliness to the subject. When one has achieved this, and *only* when one has achieved this, he should then study all the basic principles. There is no effort here to be authoritarian. No one will try to make the subject difficult.

You may have been taught that the mind, spirit and life are very difficult things to know about. This is the first principle of Scientology:

IT IS POSSIBLE TO KNOW ABOUT THE MIND, THE SPIRIT AND LIFE.

"This is the first principle of Scientology:
It is possible to know about the mind,
the spirit and life."

Chapter Two

THE CYCLE-OF-ACTION

THE
CYCLE-OF-ACTION

HE MOST FUNDAMENTAL idea in Scientology is called the CYCLE-OF-ACTION.

Cycle = a span of time with a beginning and an end = a section of the totality of time with a beginning and an end = in beginningless and endless time, one can set out periods which do have a beginning and an end insofar as action is concerned.

Action = motion or movement = an act = a consideration that motion has occurred.

In very ancient books, it is written that: From chaos came *birth*. From birth there was *growth*. When growth was achieved, there was then a gradual *decay*. The decay then ended in *death*. After death there was *chaos*.

Scientology expresses this more briefly. The cycle-of-action is an *apparency* as follows:

CREATE, then SURVIVE, then DESTROY, or

CREATION, SURVIVAL, DESTRUCTION.

First there is *creation*.

This is then followed by *survival*.

This is followed by *destruction*.

Apparency = appears to be, as distinct from what actually *is*.

This cycle is only an apparency. It is what we see, what we behold, what we believe. We consider (think, believe, suppose) that it is so and we then see it so.

A child is born, he grows, he reaches manhood, he grows old, he dies. In Scientology, it can be seen that none of these steps are necessary. One considers them so, and so they are "true." A man can grow old quickly or slowly. He grows old to the degree that he believes he is growing old. Because everyone "agrees" that this is the way things are, they go that way. The cycle is not true. It is only apparent. It is apparent because we believe we see it. It is *apparent* because we *agree* that it should be so.

The test of this principle is as follows: By using the cycle-of-action can we make anyone well or more intelligent? Thousands of tests have proven that the use of and belief in the cycle-of-action has made none well or intelligent. Therefore, no matter if we see it, there must be something wrong with it. The woman growing old, wishing to appear younger, is protesting this cycle-of-action. She feels there is something wrong with it. There is. We have to find out what the actual cycle is before we can make people better.

Actual = what is really true = that which exists despite all apparencies = that which underlies the way things seem to be = the way things really *are*.

The *actual* cycle-of-action is as follows:

CREATE, CREATE-CREATE-CREATE, CREATE-COUNTER-CREATE, NO-CREATION, NOTHINGNESS.

Create = make, manufacture, construct, postulate, bring into beingness = *Create*.

Create-Create-Create = create again continuously one moment after the next = *Survive*.

Create–Counter–Create = to create something against a creation = to create one thing and then create something else against it = *Destroy*.

No-Creation = an absence of any creation = no creative activity.

An actual cycle-of-action, then, consists of various activities, but each and every one of them is *creative*.

The cycle-of-action contains an *apparency* of *survival*, but this is *actually* only a continuous creation (create-create-create).

The *apparent* cycle-of-action contains *destruction*, but the *actual* cycle-of-action tells us what destruction is.

Destruction is one of two activities.

Destruction is (in terms of action) a creation of something against a creation of something else (create–counter–create).

For example, a wall is seen standing. To be apparent, it is necessary that the wall be constantly created. The act of "destruction" is to exert against the wall another creativeness — that is, the action or activity of knocking the wall down. Both the wall standing there and the action of knocking it down are creative actions. Because we may object to or dislike a wall being knocked down, we vilify the creativeness involved in knocking it down with the word "destructive."

Actuality tells us that there is no such thing as destruction. There is only creation against a creation.

There is another type of destruction and this is no more creation (no-creation). By no longer being a party to the wall's creation, the wall in theory can cease to exist for one. This is true in actual practice in Scientology.

Reality = the way things appear = reality is *apparency*.

To do anything about reality, one must search into and discover what underlies the apparency. Of what does reality consist (what is reality composed of)? We see an apparency which has the cycle-of-action of Create-Survive-Destroy. More basically, this cycle-of-action contains nothing but *creation*.

If one stops making something completely and ceases to be a party to its manufacture, it no longer exists for one. If one ceases to create, there is nothingness. When one creates something or beholds something which is created, that thing is still being created. Even if one is creating something with his left hand and has forgotten about it with his right hand, the thing still exists. In other words, one can create something without knowing it is still being created. Then one seeks to destroy it by a counter-creation (a creation against it). The result is a chaos created by two opposing creations.

Let us be practical. A theory is no good unless it works. All the fancy and beautiful theory in the world is useless unless it has a use or a workability. Is *this* cycle-of-action theory useful? It is. So long as we believe that we have to destroy with force in order to destroy at all, as long as we think in terms of "destruction," we have chaos.

There is creating and *knowing* one is creating.

There is creating and *not knowing* one is creating.

When one drives a car or a cart, he does many things which he is not aware of (conscious of, knowing about) and these we call "automatic actions."

One is doing something and is not aware that he is doing it. One starts to create something, then places this thought (still active) beyond his own reach and the creation continues to occur. Knowingly creating something is always the first condition. One can then purposefully continue the creation unknowingly. Everything one is doing, knowingly or unknowingly, one is doing here and now — in the present instant, in present time. One knowingly started any creation in some past moment. But the creation is being done in the present moment.

To stop any creation, it can be established that one once knew one was creating it (finding that thought) and making it known again. Or one can simply create newly and consciously what one is already creating unconsciously (unknowingly). In either case the creation stops. The *wrong* way is to start a new creation to counter against the old creation. When one does this, he gets confusion and chaos.

For example, a man has a bad leg. He is trying to get well. He seeks then to create a good leg. He goes to doctors and wants to be healed. The treatment is difficult, and usually somewhat unsuccessful, in the case of a very severely crippled leg. *Something* is creating a bad leg. Against this *he* is creating a good leg. The result is confusion and a bad leg. But a *third* creativeness is present. First something was creating, we hope, a good leg. Then a counter-creation (such as an accident to his leg) counter-created a bad leg. Now he is trying to counter-create again a good leg. The result is to wipe out the original good leg since that is the creation he is taking over and exposing with his efforts to get well. He wants a good leg. The trouble with him is the counter-creation of a bad leg. The test is factual. Have him "create (by a certain Scientology process) bad legs," until the counter-creation of bad legs is wiped out, and the original creation of a good leg will reappear. This only fails when there is no original creation of a good leg.

For example, a man has a job. He works at it. That is to say, he create-create-creates a job throughout the days, weeks and years. As long as he makes a job, the job exists. One day he depends upon (takes for granted) this job. He no longer creates it. It ceases to exist. He has no job. The apparency is that he loafed (became lazy) and was discharged. The actuality is that he no longer created a job and so didn't have one.

For example, a man depends upon a woman to keep his house for him. One day he no longer has a woman. He can't keep house even though before he married the woman he could keep house.

For example, a man is sane. He gets the idea (creates the idea) that it would be better to be insane. He starts to go insane (having created it) and then does numberless things in order to stay sane. Here, he was already creating the state of sanity, he counter-created insanity, he then counter-created sanity against insanity.

Creation in this work may be thought to exclude God. We are here considering only those things which Man or Man as a spirit can make or manufacture or think. The subject of *who* or *what* is doing the creation does not invalidate the cycle. This is a work on the subject of the mind, spirit and life, not a work on the subject of the Supreme Being.

Lying is the lowest order of creativity.

There are many tests for these principles in Scientology. Such tests come under the heading of PROCESSING.

NOTHINGNESS

CREATE

NO-CREATION

CREATE-CREATE-CREATE

CREATE–COUNTER-CREATE

"An actual cycle-of-action, then, consists of various activities, but each and every one of them is creative."

THE CONDITIONS OF EXISTENCE

The Conditions
of Existence

 HERE ARE THREE CONDITIONS-OF-EXISTENCE. These three conditions comprise (make up, constitute) life.

They are BE, DO and HAVE.

The first condition of existence is BEING.

Being is defined as "the assumption (choosing) of a category of identity." It could be said to be the role in a game.

An example of beingness could be one's own name. Another example would be one's profession. Another example would be one's physical characteristics. Each or all of these things could be called one's beingness.

Beingness is assumed by oneself, or given to oneself, or is attained.

For example, in the playing of a game each player has his own beingness.

The second condition of existence is DOING.

By doing we mean "action, function, accomplishment, the attainment of goals, the fulfilling of purpose, or any change of position in space."

The third condition of existence is HAVINGNESS.

By havingness we mean "owning, possessing, being capable of commanding, positioning, taking charge of objects, energies or spaces." The essential definition of having is "to be able to touch, or permeate, or to direct the disposition of."

The game of life demands that one assumes a *beingness* in order to accomplish a *doingness* in the direction of *havingness*.

These three conditions are given in an order of seniority (importance) where life is concerned. The ability to be is more important than the ability to do. The ability to do is more important than the ability to have. In most people all three conditions are sufficiently confused that they are best understood in reverse order. When one has clarified the idea of havingness (or possession), one can then proceed to clarify doingness (or general activity) and when this is done one understands beingness (or identity).

It is essential to a successful existence that each of these three conditions be clarified and understood. The ability to assume or to grant (give, allow) beingness is probably the highest of human virtues. It is even more important to be able to permit other people to have beingness than to be able, oneself, to assume it.

"The game of life demands
that one assumes a beingness
in order to accomplish a doingness
in the direction of havingness."

THE
EIGHT DYNAMICS

THE
EIGHT DYNAMICS

S ONE LOOKS out across the confusion which is life or existence to most people, one can discover eight main divisions to each of which apply the *conditions-of-existence*. Each division also contains a *cycle-of-action*.

There could be said to be eight urges (drives, impulses) in life.

These we call DYNAMICS.

These are motives or motivations.

We call them THE EIGHT DYNAMICS.

There is no thought or statement here that any one of these eight dynamics is more important than the others. While they are categories (divisions) of the broad game of life, they are not necessarily equal to each other. It will be found amongst individuals that each person stresses one of the dynamics more than the others, or may stress a combination of dynamics as more important than other combinations.

The purpose in setting forth this division is to increase an understanding of life by placing it in compartments. Having subdivided existence in this fashion, each compartment can be inspected (as itself and by itself) in its relationship to the other compartments of life.

In working a puzzle, it is necessary to first take pieces of similar color or character and place them in groups. In studying a subject, it is necessary to proceed in an orderly fashion.

To promote this orderliness, it is necessary to assume (for our purposes) these eight arbitrary compartments of life.

THE FIRST DYNAMIC – is the urge toward existence as one's self. Here we have individuality expressed fully. This can be called the *Self Dynamic*.

THE SECOND DYNAMIC – is the urge toward existence as a sexual activity. This dynamic actually has two divisions. Second Dynamic (a) is the sexual act itself. And the Second Dynamic (b) is the family unit, including the rearing of children. This can be called the *Sex Dynamic*.

THE THIRD DYNAMIC – is the urge toward existence in groups of individuals. Any group, or part of an entire class, could be considered to be a part of the Third Dynamic. The school, the society, the town, the nation are each *part* of the Third Dynamic and each one *is* a Third Dynamic. This can be called the *Group Dynamic*.

THE FOURTH DYNAMIC – is the urge toward existence as or of Mankind. Whereas one race would be considered a Third Dynamic, all the races would be considered the Fourth Dynamic. This can be called the *Mankind Dynamic*.

THE FIFTH DYNAMIC – is the urge toward existence of the animal kingdom. This includes all living things, whether vegetable or animal, the fish in the sea, the beasts of the field or of the forest, grass, trees, flowers or anything directly and intimately motivated by *life*. This can be called the *Animal Dynamic*.

THE SIXTH DYNAMIC – is the urge toward existence as the physical universe. The physical universe is composed of Matter, Energy, Space and Time. In Scientology we take the first letter of each of these words and coin a word – MEST. This can be called the *Universe Dynamic*.

THE SEVENTH DYNAMIC – is the urge toward existence as or of spirits. Anything spiritual, with or without identity, would come under the heading of the Seventh Dynamic. This can be called the *Spiritual Dynamic*.

THE EIGHTH DYNAMIC – is the urge toward existence as infinity. This is also identified as the Supreme Being. This is called the Eighth Dynamic because the symbol of infinity, ∞, stood upright makes the numeral 8. This can be called the *Infinity* or *God Dynamic*.

Scientologists usually call these by number.

The earlier subject, Dianetics, included dynamics one to four. Scientology embraces dynamics one through seven as known territory, scientifically demonstrated and classified.

The difficulty of stating the exact definitions of the dynamics is entirely verbal. Originally, the dynamics read "the urge towards *survival* as _____." As the subject developed, it became apparent that survival was only an *apparency* and only one facet of existence.

Both the cycle-of-action and the three conditions-of-existence belong in each dynamic.

A further manifestation of these dynamics is that they could best be represented as a series of concentric circles, wherein the First Dynamic would be the center and each new dynamic would be successively a circle outside it. The idea of space expanding enters into these dynamics.

The basic characteristic of the individual includes his ability to so expand into the other dynamics. But when the Seventh Dynamic is reached in its entirety, one will only then discover the true Eighth Dynamic.

As an example of use of these dynamics, one discovers that a baby at birth is not perceptive beyond the First Dynamic. But as the child grows and interests extend, the child can be seen to embrace other dynamics.

As a further example of use, a person who is incapable of operating on the Third Dynamic is incapable at once of being a part of a team and so might be said to be incapable of a social existence.

As a further comment upon the eight dynamics, no one of these dynamics from one to seven is more important than any other one of them in terms of orienting the individual. While the dynamics are not of equal importance, one to the next, the ability of an individual to assume the beingness, doingness and havingness of each dynamic is an index to his ability to live.

The eight dynamics are used in Scientology communication and should be perfectly learned as part of the language of Scientology. The abilities and shortcomings of individuals can be understood by viewing their participation in the various dynamics.

"A further manifestation
of these dynamics is that they could
best be represented as a series of concentric
circles, wherein the First Dynamic would be
the center and each new dynamic would be
successively a circle outside it."

THE
A-R-C TRIANGLE

GUIDE TO THE MATERIALS

YOU'RE ON AN ADVENTURE!
HERE'S THE MAP.

Your journey to a full understanding of Dianetics and Scientology is the greatest adventure of all. But you need a map that shows you where you are and where you are going.

To obtain your **FREE Materials Guide Chart and Catalog,** fill out the following information and drop this card in the mail.

NAME _____

ADDRESS _____

CITY _____ BOOK THIS CARD CAME IN _____

STATE/PROVINCE _____

PHONE _____ ZIP/POSTAL CODE _____

E-MAIL _____

www.bridgepub.com

BUSINESS REPLY MAIL

FIRST-CLASS MAIL PERMIT NO. 62688 LOS ANGELES CA

POSTAGE WILL BE PAID BY ADDRESSEE

BRIDGE PUBLICATIONS, INC.
4751 FOUNTAIN AVE
LOS ANGELES CA 90029-9949

THE
A-R-C TRIANGLE

HERE IS A TRIANGLE of considerable importance in Scientology, and an ability to use it gives a much greater understanding of life.

The A-R-C TRIANGLE is the keystone of living associations. This triangle is the common denominator to all of life's activities.

The first corner of the triangle is called AFFINITY.

The basic definition of affinity is "the consideration of distance, whether good or bad." The most basic function of complete affinity would be the ability to occupy the same space as something else.

The word affinity is here used to mean "love, liking or any other emotional attitude." Affinity is conceived in Scientology to be something of many facets. Affinity is a variable quality. Affinity is here used as a word with the context "degree of liking."

Under affinity we have the various emotional tones, ranged from the highest to the lowest, and these are in part:

Serenity (the highest level)

Enthusiasm

Conservatism (as we proceed downward towards the baser affinities)

Boredom

Antagonism

Anger

Covert Hostility

Fear

Grief

Apathy

(This, in Scientology, is called the TONE SCALE.)

Below Apathy, affinity proceeds into solidities such as matter. Affinity is conceived to be comprised first of thought, then of emotion which contains energy particles, and then as a solid.

The second corner of the triangle is REALITY.

Reality could be defined as "that which appears to be." Reality is fundamentally agreement. What we agree to be real is real.

The third corner of the triangle is COMMUNICATION.

In understanding the composition of human relations in this universe, communication is more important than the other two corners of the triangle. Communication is the solvent for all things (it dissolves all things).

The interrelationship of the triangle becomes apparent at once when one asks, "Have you ever tried to talk to an angry man?" Without a high degree of liking and without some basis of agreement, there is no *communication*. Without communication and some basis of emotional response, there can be no *reality*. Without some basis for agreement and communication, there can be no *affinity*. Thus we call these three things a *triangle*. Unless we have two corners of a triangle, there cannot be a third corner. Desiring any corner of the triangle, one must include the other two.

The triangle is conceived to be very spacious at the level of Serenity and completely condensed at the level of matter. Thus, to represent a scale for use, one would draw a large triangle with the high part of the scale and succeedingly smaller triangles down to a dot at the bottom of the scale.

Affinity, Reality and Communication are the basis of the Scientology Tone Scale which gives a prediction of human behavior.*

As has already been noted, the triangle is not an equilateral (all sides the same) triangle. Affinity and reality are very much less important than communication. It might be said that the triangle begins with communication which brings into existence affinity and reality.

*The Tone Scale, its complete description and use, is contained in *Science of Survival*.

A-R-C *are* UNDERSTANDING.

If you would continue a strong and able communication with someone, there must be some basis for agreement, there must be some liking for the person and then communication can exist. We can see, then, that simple "talking" and "writing" randomly, without knowledge of this, would not necessarily be communication. Communication is essentially "something which is sent and which is received." The intention to send and the intention to receive must both be present, in some degree, before an actual communication can take place. Therefore, one could have conditions which appear to be communications which were not.*

Original with Scientology (as are all these concepts), the A-R-C Triangle, understood, is an extremely useful tool or weapon in human relationships. For instance, amongst the A-R-C Triangle laws, a communication to be received must approximate the affinity level of the person to whom it is directed. As people descend the Tone Scale, they become more and more difficult to communicate with and things with which they will agree become more and more solid. Thus, we have friendly discourses high on the scale and war at the bottom. Where the affinity level is hate, the agreement is solid matter, and the communication...*bullets*.

*The complete manual of communication is *Dianetics 55!*

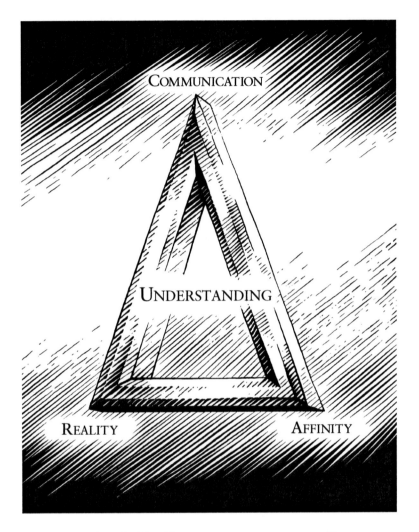

"A-R-C are understanding."

THE
REASON WHY

Chapter Six

THE REASON WHY

LIFE CAN BEST be understood by likening it to a GAME.

Since we are exterior to a great number of games, we can regard them with a detached eye. If we were exterior to life, instead of being involved and immersed in the living of it, it would look to us much like games look to us from our present vantage point.

Despite the amount of suffering, pain, misery, sorrow and travail which can exist in life, the reason for existence is the same reason as one has to play a game — interest, contest, activity and possession. The truth of this assertion is established by an observation of the elements of games and then applying these elements to life itself. When we do this, we find nothing left wanting in the panorama of life.

By game we mean "contest of person against person, or team against team." When we say games, we mean such games as baseball, polo, chess or any other such pastime.

It may at one time have struck you peculiar that men would risk bodily injury in the field of play, just for the sake of "amusement." So it might strike you as peculiar that people would go on living or would enter into the "game of life," at the risk of all the sorrow, travail and pain, just to have "something to do." Evidently there is no greater curse than total idleness. Of course, there is that condition where a person continues to play a game in which he is no longer interested.

If you will but look about the room and check off items in which you are not interested, you will discover something remarkable. In a short time, you will find that there is nothing in the room in which you are not interested. You are interested in everything. However, disinterest itself is one of the mechanisms of play. In order to hide something, it is only necessary to make everyone disinterested in the place where the item is hidden. Disinterest is not an immediate result of interest which has worn out. Disinterest is a commodity in itself. It is palpable. It exists.

By studying the elements of games, we find ourselves in possession of the elements of life.

LIFE IS A GAME.

A game consists of FREEDOM, BARRIERS and PURPOSES.

This is a scientific fact, not merely an observation.

Freedom exists amongst barriers. A totality of barriers and a totality of freedom, alike, are "no-game conditions." Each is similarly cruel. Each is similarly purposeless.

Great revolutionary movements fail. They promise unlimited freedom. That is the road to failure. Only stupid visionaries chant of endless freedom. Only the afraid and ignorant speak of and insist upon unlimited barriers.

When the relation between freedom and barriers becomes too unbalanced, an unhappiness results.

"Freedom from" is all right only so long as there is a place to be free *to*. An endless desire for "freedom from" is a perfect trap, a fear of all things.

Barriers are composed of inhibiting (limiting) ideas, space, energy, masses and time. Freedom, in its entirety, would be a total absence of these things. But it would also be a freedom without thought or action – an unhappy condition of total nothingness.

Fixed on too many barriers, Man yearns to be free. But launched into total freedom, he is purposeless and miserable.

There is "freedom amongst" barriers. If the barriers are known and the freedoms are known, there can be life, living, happiness, a game.

The restrictions of a government or a job give an employee his freedom. Without known restrictions, an employee is a slave doomed to the fears of uncertainty in all his actions.

Executives in business and government can fail in three ways and thus bring about a chaos in their department. They can:

1. Seem to give endless freedom.

2. Seem to give endless barriers.

3. Make neither freedom nor barriers certain.

Executive competence, therefore, consists of imposing and enforcing an adequate balance between their people's freedom and the unit's barriers *and* in being precise and consistent about those freedoms and barriers. Such an executive, adding only in himself initiative and purpose, can have a department with initiative and purpose.

An employee buying and/or insisting upon "freedom only" will become a slave. Knowing the above facts, he must insist upon a workable balance between freedom and barriers.

An examination of the dynamics (Chapter Four) will demonstrate the possibility of a combination of teams. Two Group Dynamics can engage one another as teams. The Self Dynamic can ally itself with the Animal Dynamic against, let us say, the Universe Dynamic and so have a game. In other words, the dynamics are an outline of possible teams and interplays. As everyone is engaged in several games, an examination of the dynamics will plot and clarify for him the various teams he is playing upon and those he is playing against. If an individual can discover that he is only playing on the Self Dynamic and that he belongs to no other team, it is certain that this individual will lose. For he has before him seven remaining dynamics and the Self Dynamic is seldom capable of besting, by itself, all the remaining dynamics. In Scientology, we call this condition the "only one." Here is Self-determinism in the guise of *Selfish*-determinism. And here is an individual who will most certainly be overwhelmed. To enjoy life, one must be willing to be some part of life.

There is the principle in Scientology called PAN-DETERMINISM.

This could be loosely defined as "determining the activities of two or more sides in a game simultaneously."

For instance, a person playing chess is being Self-determined and is playing chess against an opponent. A person who is Pan-determined on the subject of chess could play both sides of the board.

A being is Pan-determined about any game to which he is *senior*. He is Self-determined only in a game to which he is *junior*.

For instance, a general of an army is Pan-determined concerning an argument between two privates or even two companies of his command. He is Pan-determined in this case. But when he confronts another army, led by another general, he becomes Self-determined. The game, in this wise, could be said to be *larger* than himself. The game becomes even larger than this when the general seeks to play the parts of all the political heads which should be above him. This is the main reason why dictatorship doesn't work. It is all but impossible for one man to be Pan-determined about the entire system of games which comprise a nation. He starts "taking sides" and then, to that degree, becomes much *less* than the government which he is seeking to run.

It has been stylish in past ages to insist only upon freedom. The French Revolution furnishes an excellent example for this. In the late part of the eighteenth century, the nobles of France became so Self-determined against the remainder of the country, and were so incapable of taking the parts of the populace, that the nobles were destroyed. Immediately, the populace itself sought to take over the government. And being untrained and being intensely antipathetic to any and all restraints, their war cry became "Freedom!" They had no further restrictions or barriers. The rules of government were thrown aside. Theft and brigandage took the place of economics. The populace, therefore, found itself in a deeper trap and discovered itself to be involved with a dictatorship which was far more restrictive than anything they had experienced before the revolution.

Although Man continually uses "Freedom!" for his war cry, he only succeeds in establishing further entrapment for himself. The reason for this is a very simple one. A game consists of freedom *and* barriers *and* purposes. When Man drops the idea of restrictions or barriers, he loses at once *control* over barriers. He becomes Self-determined about barriers and not Pan-determined. Thus, he cannot control the barriers. The barriers, left uncontrolled, trap him then and there.

The "dwindling spiral" of the apparency, Create-Survive-Destroy, comes about directly when Man shuns barriers. If he considers all restrictions and barriers his enemies, he is of course refusing to control them in any way and thus he starts his own dwindling spiral.

A race which is educated to think in terms of "freedom only" is very easily entrapped. No one in the nation will take responsibility for restrictions. Therefore, restrictions apparently become less and less. Actually, they become more and more. As these restrictions lessen, so lessens the freedom of the individual. One cannot be free from a wall unless there is a wall. Lacking any restrictions, life becomes purposeless, random, chaotic.

A good manager must be capable of taking responsibility for restrictions. In that freedom, to exist, must have barriers, a failure to take initiative on the subject of restrictions or barriers causes them to arise all by themselves and exist without consent or direction.

There are various states of mind which bring about happiness. That state of mind which insists only upon freedom can bring about nothing but unhappiness. It would be better to develop a thought pattern which looked for new ways to be entrapped and things to be trapped in, than to suffer the eventual total entrapment of dwelling upon "freedom only." A man who is willing to accept restrictions and barriers and is not afraid of them is *free*. A man who does nothing but fight restrictions and barriers will usually be *trapped*. The way to have endless war is "abandon" all war.

As it can be seen in any game, purposes become counterposed. There is a matter of purpose-counter-purpose in almost any game played in a field with two teams. One team has the idea of reaching the goal of the other, and the other has the idea of reaching the goal of the first. Their purposes are at war and this warring of purposes makes a game.

The war of purposes gives us what we call PROBLEMS.

A problem has the anatomy of purposes. A problem consists of two or more purposes opposed. It does not matter what problem you face or have faced, the basic anatomy of that problem is purpose-counter-purpose.

In actual testing, in Scientology, it has been discovered that a person begins to suffer from problems when he does not have enough of them. There is the old saw (maxim) that if you want a thing done, give it to a busy man to do. Similarly, if you want a happy associate, make sure that he is a man who can have lots of problems.

From this we get the oddity of a high incidence of neurosis in the families of the rich. These people have very little to do and have very few problems. The basic problems of food, clothing and shelter are already solved for them. We would suppose, then, if it were true that an individual's happiness depended only upon his freedom, these people would be happy. However, they are not happy. What brings about their unhappiness? It is the lack of problems.

Although successful processing in Scientology would depend upon taking all three elements of games into consideration (and, indeed, that is the secret of bettering people – taking freedom, barriers and purposes into consideration and balancing them), it is true that you could make a man well simply by sitting down with him and asking him to "invent problems" one after the other. The invention of synthetic problems would be found to free his mind and make him more able. Of course, there is another factor involved in this: In that it is *he* who is inventing the problems, he is therefore becoming Pan-determined about problems rather than being in one place with all problems opposed to him.

An unhappy man is one who is considering, continually, how to become free. One sees this in the clerk who is continually trying to avoid work. Although he has a great deal of leisure time, he is not enjoying any part of it. He is trying to avoid contact with people, objects, energies and spaces. He eventually becomes trapped in a sort of lethargy. If this man could merely change his mind and start "worrying" about how he could get more work to do, his happiness level would increase markedly.

One who is plotting continually how to "get out of things" will become miserable. One who is plotting how to "get into things" has a much better chance of becoming happy.

There is, of course, the matter of being forced to play games in which one has no interest. A war into which one is drafted is an excellent example of this. One is not interested in the purposes of the war and yet one finds himself fighting it. Thus there must be an additional element.

And this element is THE POWER OF CHOICE.

One could say, then, that life is a game and that the ability to play a game consists of tolerance for freedom and barriers and an insight into purposes with the power of choice over participation.

These four elements — *freedom, barriers, purposes* and *power of choice* — are the guiding elements of life. There are only two factors above these and both of them are related to these. The first is the ability to *create* with, of course, its negative, the ability to *uncreate*. And the second is the ability to make a *postulate* (to consider, to say a thing, and have it be true).

This, then, is the broad picture of life. And in bringing life into focus and in making it less confusing, these elements are used in its understanding.

"One could say, then, that life is a game
and that the ability to play a game
consists of tolerance for freedom
and barriers and an insight into purposes
with the power of choice over participation."

THE
PARTS OF MAN

Chapter Seven

THE

PARTS OF MAN

 HE INDIVIDUAL MAN is divisible into three parts.

The first of these is the spirit, called in Scientology the THETAN.

The second of these parts is the MIND.

The third of these parts is the BODY.

Probably the greatest discovery of Scientology, and its most forceful contribution to the knowledge of Mankind, has been the isolation, description and handling of the human spirit. Accomplished in July 1952 in Phoenix, Arizona, I established along scientific lines (rather than mere belief) that: That thing which is the person, the personality, is separable from the body and the mind at will and without causing bodily death or mental derangement.

In ages past, there has been considerable controversy concerning the human spirit or soul. And various attempts to control Man have been effective in view of his almost complete ignorance of his own identity.

Latterly, spiritualists isolated from the person what they called the "astral body." And with this, they were able to work for various purposes of their own. In Scientology, the spirit itself was separated from what the spiritualists called the astral body and there should be no confusion between these two things. As you know that you are where you are at this moment, so you would know if you, a spirit, were detached from your mind and body. Man has not discovered this before because, lacking the technologies of Scientology, he had very little reality upon his detachment from his mind and body. Therefore he conceived himself to be, at least in part, a mind and a body. The entire cult of communism is based upon the fact that one lives only one life, that there is no Hereafter and that the individual has no religious significance. Man, at large, has been close to this state for at least the last century. The state (condition) is of a very low order excluding, as it does, all self-recognition.

THE SPIRIT

The THETAN (spirit) is described in Scientology as having no mass, no wavelength, no energy and no time or location in space, except by consideration or postulate.

The spirit, then, is not a *thing*. It is the *creator* of things.

The usual residence of the thetan is in the skull or near the body. A thetan can be in one of four conditions:

1. The first would be entirely separate from a body or bodies, or even from this universe.

2. The second would be near a body and knowingly controlling the body.

3. The third would be in the body (the skull).

4. And the fourth would be an inverted condition, whereby he is compulsively away from the body and cannot approach it.

There are degrees (subdivisions) of each one of these four states. The most optimum of these conditions, from the standpoint of Man, is the second.

A thetan is subject to deterioration. This is at first difficult to understand, since the entirety of his activity consists of *considering* or *postulating*. He uses, through his postulates, various methods of controlling a body. That he does deteriorate is manifest. But that he can at any moment return to an entirety of his ability is also factual. In that he associates beingness with mass and action, he does not consider himself as having an individual identity or name unless he is connected with one or more of the games of life.

The processes of Scientology can establish this for the individual with greater or lesser rapidity. And one of the many goals of processing in Scientology is to "exteriorize" the individual and place him in the second condition above (near a body and knowingly controlling the body), since it has been discovered that he is happier and more capable when so situated.

THE MIND

The MIND is a communication and control system between the thetan and his environment. A thetan establishes various systems of control so that he can continue to operate a body and, through the body, operate things in the physical universe as well as other bodies. The most obvious portion of the mind is recognizable by anyone not in serious condition. This is the "mental image picture." In Scientology, we call this mental image picture a *facsimile* when it is a "photograph" of the physical universe some time in the past. We call this mental image picture a *mock-up* when it is created by the thetan, or for the thetan, and does not consist of a photograph of the physical universe. We call a mental image picture a "hallucination" or, more properly, an *automaticity* (something uncontrolled) when it is created by another and seen by self.

Various phenomena connect themselves with this entity called the mind. Some people, closing their eyes, see only blackness. Some people see pictures. Some people see pictures made by body reactions. Some people see only black screens. Others see golden lines. Others see spaces. But the keynote of the entirety of the system called the mind is *postulate* and *perception*. Easily ten thousand new, separate mental phenomena, not hitherto seen by earlier observers, have been classified in Scientology and Dianetics (that branch of Scientology which applies only to the mind).

The thetan receives, by the communication system called the mind, various impressions including direct views of the physical universe. In addition to this, he receives impressions from past activities and, most important, he himself being close to a total knowingness, conceives things about the past and future which are independent of immediately present stimuli. The mind is not, in its entirety, a stimulus-response mechanism (as old Marxist psychology, as once taught in universities, would have one believe).

The mind has three main divisions:

The first of these could be called the ANALYTICAL MIND.

The second, the REACTIVE MIND.

And the third, the SOMATIC MIND.

The Analytical Mind

The ANALYTICAL MIND combines perceptions of the *immediate* environment, of the *past* (via pictures) and estimations of the *future,* into conclusions which are based upon the realities of situations. The analytical mind combines the potential knowingness of the thetan with the conditions of his surroundings and brings him to independent conclusions. This mind could be said to consist of visual pictures, either of the past or the physical universe, monitored by and presided over by the knowingness of a thetan.

The keynote of the analytical mind is *awareness*—one knows what one is concluding and knows what he is doing.

The Reactive Mind

The REACTIVE MIND is a stimulus-response mechanism. Ruggedly built and operable in trying circumstances, the reactive mind *never* stops operating. Pictures of a very low order are taken by this mind of the environment, even in some states of unconsciousness. The reactive mind acts *below* the level of consciousness. *It* is the literal stimulus-response mind. Given a certain stimulus, it gives a certain response.

The entire subject of Dianetics concerned itself mainly with this one mind.

While it is an order of "thinkingness," the ability of the reactive mind to conclude rationally is so poor that we find in the reactive mind those various aberrated impulses which are gazed upon as oddities of personality, eccentricities, neuroses and psychoses. It is this mind which stores up all the bad things that have happened to one and throws them back to him again, in moments of emergency or danger, so as to dictate his actions along lines which have been considered "safe" before. As there is little thinkingness involved in this, the courses of action dictated by the reactive mind are often not safe, but highly dangerous.

The reactive mind is entirely *literal* in its "interpretation" of words and actions. As it takes pictures and receives impressions during moments of unconsciousness, a phrase uttered when a blow is struck is likely to be literally interpreted by the reactive mind and become active upon the body and analytical mind at later times.

The mildest stage of this would be arduous training, wherein a pattern is laid into the mind for later use under certain given stimuli.

A harsher and less workable level is the hypnotic trance condition to which the mind is susceptible. Made impressionable by fixed attention, words can be immediately implanted into the reactive mind which become operable under "restimulation" at later times.

An even lower level in the reactive mind is that one associated with blows, drugs, illness, pain and other conditions of unconsciousness. Phrases spoken over an anesthetized person can have a later effect upon that person. It is not necessarily true that each and every portion of an operation is painstakingly "photographed" by the reactive mind of the unconscious patient. But it is true that a great many of these stimuli are registered. Complete silence in the vicinity of a person under anesthetic, or a person who is unconscious or in deep pain, is mandatory if one would preserve the mental health of that person or patient afterwards.

Probably the most therapeutic action which could occur to an individual would be, under Scientology processing, the separation of the thetan from the mind so that the thetan, under no duress and with total knowingness, could view himself and his mind and act accordingly.

However, there is a type of exteriorization which is the most aberrative of all traumatic (mentally injurious) actions. This is the condition when an individual is brought, through injury or surgery or shock, very close to death so that he exteriorizes from body and mind. This exteriorization under duress is sudden and, to the patient, inexplicable, and is in itself very shocking. When this has occurred to an individual, it is certain that he will suffer mentally from the experience afterwards. It could be said that when the reactive mind contains these sudden shocks of exteriorization under duress, attempts to exteriorize the individual later, by Scientology, are more difficult. However, modern processing has overcome this.

The phenomenon of exteriorization under duress is accompanied at times by energy explosions in the various facsimiles of the mind and these cross-associate in the reactive mind. Therefore, people become afraid of exteriorization and, at times, are made ill simply by discussing the phenomenon due to the fact that they have exteriorized under duress during some operation or accident. Exteriorization under duress is the characteristic of death itself. Therefore exteriorization, or the departure of the soul, is generally associated with death in the minds of most people. It is not necessarily true that one is dead because he exteriorizes. And it is definitely not true that exteriorization not accompanied by a shock, pain or duress is at all painful. Indeed, it is quite therapeutic.

The Somatic Mind

The third portion of the mind is the SOMATIC MIND. This is an even heavier type of mind than the reactive mind, since it contains no "thinkingness" and contains only "actingness." The impulses placed against the body by the thetan, through various mental machinery, arrive at the voluntary, involuntary and glandular levels. These have set methods of analysis for any given situation and so respond directly to commands given.

Unfortunately, the somatic mind is subject to each of the minds higher in scale above it and to the thetan. In other words, the thetan can independently affect the somatic mind. The analytical mind can affect the somatic mind. The reactive mind can affect the somatic mind. Thus we see that the neurons, the glandular system, the muscles and masses of the body are subject to various impulses, each one of a lower order than the next. Thus it is not odd to discover what we call "psychosomatic" illness. A condition exists here where the thetan does not have an awareness of burdening the somatic mind with various commands or derangements. Neither does the thetan have an awareness of his own participation in the analytical mind causing this action against the body.

In that the thetan is seldom aware of the reactive mind, it is possible then for the reactive mind (with its stimulus-response content) to impinge itself directly, and without further recourse or advice, upon the neurons, muscles and glandular system of the body. In that the reactive mind can hold a fixed "command" in place, causing a derangement in the somatic mind, it is possible then for illness to exist, for bizarre pains to be felt, for actual physical twists and aberrations to occur without any conscious knowledge on the part of the thetan. This we call "physical illness caused by the mind." In brief, such illness is caused by perceptions received in the reactive mind during moments of pain and unconsciousness.

Whether the facsimile in the mind is received while the thetan is awake or unconscious, the resulting mass of the "energy picture" is *energy* – just as you see energy in an electric light bulb or from the flames of a fire. At one time it was considered that "mental energy" was different from "physical energy." In Scientology it has been discovered that mental energy is simply a finer, higher-level physical energy.

The test of this is conclusive in that a thetan, mocking-up (creating) mental image pictures and thrusting them into the body, can increase the body mass. And, by casting them away again, can decrease the body mass. This test has actually been made and an increase of as much as thirty pounds (actually measured on scales) has been added to and subtracted from a body by creating mental energy.

Energy is energy. It has different wavelengths and different characteristics. The mental image pictures are capable of reacting upon the physical environment, and the physical environment is capable of reacting upon mental image pictures.

Thus, the mind actually consists of spaces, energies and masses of the same order as the physical universe – if lighter and different in size and wavelength.

For a much more comprehensive picture of the mind, one should read *Dianetics: The Original Thesis* and *Dianetics: The Modern Science of Mental Health.* These were written before the discovery of the upper levels of beingness were made and are a very complete picture of the mind itself, its structure and what can be done to it and with it.

THE BODY

The third part of Man is the physical BODY. This can best be studied in such books as *Gray's Anatomy* and other anatomical texts. This is the province of the medical doctor and, usually, the old-time psychiatrist or psychologist (who were involved, in the main, in "body worship"). The body is a purely structural study and the actions and reactions amongst its various structures are complex and intensely interesting.

When Scientology established biophysics, it did so because of the various discoveries which had accumulated concerning mental energy in its reaction against physical energy and the activities which took place in the body because of these interactions. Biophysics only became feasible when it was discovered in Scientology that a fixed electrical field existed surrounding a body, entirely independent of but influenceable by the human mind. The body exists in its own space. That space is created by *anchor points* (points which are anchored in a space different to the physical universe space around a body). The complexity of these anchor points can cause an independent series of electronic flows which can occasion much discomfort to the individual. The balance structure of the body, and even its joint action and physical characteristics, can be changed by changing this electrical field which exists at a distance from or within the body.

The electrical field is paramount and monitors the actual physical structure of the body. Thus, the body is not only influenced by the three minds, it is influenced as well by its own electrical field.

(An expert Scientologist can discover this field for the average person and can bring about its adjustment, although this is very far from the primary purpose of the Scientologist.)

The use of electrical shocks upon a body, for any purpose, is therefore very dangerous and is not condoned by sensible men. Of course, the use of electrical shock was never intended to be therapeutic, but was intended only to bring about "obedience" by duress and (as far as it can be discovered) to make the entirety of insanity a horror. Electrical shock deranges the electronic field in the vicinity of the body and is *always* succeeded by bad health or physical difficulties and *never* does otherwise than hasten the death of the person. It has been stated by people using electric shock that if they were denied euthanasia (the right to kill people who were considered to be a burden on a society), they would at least use "partial euthanasia" in the form of electric shock, brain surgery and drugs. These "treatments" in some large percentage of cases, however, effected euthanasia—as they were *expected* to do.

A knowledge of the mental *and* physical structure of the body would be necessary in order to treat the body. And this knowledge has not existed prior to Scientology. The medical doctor achieved many results by working purely with structure and biochemical products. And in the field of emergency surgery and obstetrics and orthopedics, he is indispensable in the society. Medicine, however, did not even contain a definition for "mind" and is not expected to invade the field which belongs, properly, to Scientology.

These three Parts of Man—the *thetan,* the *mind* and the *body*—are each one different studies, but they influence each other markedly and continually. Of the three, the senior entity is the thetan. For without the thetan, there would be no mind or animation in the body. While without a body or a mind, there is still animation and life in the thetan.

The thetan *is* the person. You are YOU *in* a body.

"These three Parts of Man—the thetan,
the mind and the body—are each one different
studies, but they influence each other
markedly and continually. Of the three,
the senior entity is the thetan."

PARA-SCIENTOLOGY

Many speculations have been made in the field of PARA-SCIENTOLOGY.

Para-Scientology includes all of the uncertainties and unknown territories of life which have not been completely explored and explained. However, as studies have gone forward, it has become more and more apparent that the senior activity of life is that of the thetan and that in the absence of the spirit no further life exists. In the insect kingdom, it is not established whether or not each insect is ordered by a spirit or whether one spirit orders enormous numbers of insects. It is not established how mutation and evolution occur (if they do). And the general Authorship of the physical universe is only speculated upon, since Scientology does not invade the Eighth Dynamic. (See Chapter Four, The Eight Dynamics.)

Some facts, however, are completely known:

1. The first of these is that the individual, himself, is a spirit controlling a body via a mind.

2. The second of these is that the thetan is capable of making space, energy, mass and time.

3. The third of these is that the thetan is separable from the body without the phenomenon of death and can handle and control a body from well outside it.

4. The fourth of these is that the thetan does not care to remember the life which he has just lived after he has parted from the body and the mind.

5. The fifth of these is that a person dying always exteriorizes.

6. The sixth of these is that the person, having exteriorized, usually returns to a planet and procures, usually, another body of the same type of race as before.

In Para-Scientology there is much discussion about "between-lives areas" and other phenomena which might have passed at one time or another for Heaven or Hell. But it is established completely that a thetan is immortal and that he, himself, cannot actually experience death and counterfeits it by "forgetting." It is adequately manifest that a thetan lives again and that he is very anxious to put something on the time track (something for the future) in order to have something to come back to. Thus we have the anxieties of sex—there must be additional bodies for the next life. It is obvious that what we create in our societies during this lifetime affects us during our next lifetime. This is quite different than the "belief" or the "idea" that this occurs. In Scientology, we have very little to do with forcing people to make conclusions. An individual can experience these things for himself. And unless he can do so, no one expects him to accept them.

The manifestation that our Hereafter is our "next life" entirely alters the general concept of spiritual destiny. There is no argument whatever with the tenets of any faith, since it is not precisely stated uniformly by all religions that one immediately goes to a Heaven or Hell. It is certain that an individual experiences the effect of the civilization, which he has had part in creating, in his next lifetime. In other words, the individual comes back. He has a responsibility for what goes on today since he will experience it tomorrow.

Sex has been overweighted in importance in old psychotherapy, an importance more or less disgraced at this time. Sex is only one of numerous creative impulses. An anxiety about sex, however, occurs when an individual begins to believe that there will not be a body for him to have during the next lifetime. The common denominator of all aberration is "cessation of creation." As sex is only one kind of creation, and a rather low order of it, it will be seen that unhappiness could stem from various cessations of creation.

Death, itself, is a cessation of creation. One stops creating the identity "John Jones" and the environment and things of "John Jones." He stops because he believes he cannot, himself, continue this creation without the assistance of a body. Having become dependent upon a mind and a body, the first to do his thinking for him and the second to do his acting, an individual becomes sufficiently morose on the ideas of creation that he can actually bring about the condition of an "inability to create."

CONTROL

It will be seen that the three Parts of Man are intimately associated with CONTROL.

The anatomy of control is START-CHANGE-and-STOP.

The loss of control takes place with the loss of Pan-determinism. When one becomes too partisan, braces himself too solidly against the remainder of the environment, he no longer controls the environment to the degree that he might and so is unable to start, change and stop the environment.

It is a scientific definition in Scientology that control consists of Start-Change-and-Stop. These three manifestations can be graphed alongside of the apparent cycle-of-action, Create-Survive-Destroy. Any person is somewhere along this curve:

An individual who is bent mainly upon *survival* is intent usually upon *changing* things.

An individual who is close to being *destroyed* is bent mainly upon *stopping* things.

An individual who has a *free* heart and mind about life is bent upon *creating* things.

There could be three things wrong with any person and these would be the inability to start, the inability to change, the inability to stop.

Insanity, for the most part, is an inability to stop. A neurosis is a "habit" which, worsening, flies entirely out of control. One is stopped so often in life that he becomes an enemy of stopping. And dislikes stopping so intensely, that he himself will not stop things. Neurosis and psychosis, of all classes, are entirely inabilities to start, to change, or to stop.

In the matter of the Parts of Man, we discover that all things are initiated by the thetan so far as action, activity and behavior are concerned. After such an initiation, he can be blunted or warped from course and acted upon in such a way that his attention becomes too fixed, along one line or another, and he begins to suffer from these three inabilities. However, each one of the Parts of Man is subject to the anatomy of control. An individual begins, first, by being unable himself (and without help) to start, to change and to stop. Then, the mind may become prone to these disabilities and is unable to start, change or stop at will. Then, the body itself can become subject to these three disabilities and is unable to start, to change and to stop.

The oddity, however, is that an environment can so work upon an individual that a thetan's body becomes disabled through no choice of his own. Similarly, the mind can become disabled through no choice of either the body or the thetan. But the thetan himself, beyond observing the effect of various causes and having initiated the thought to be there, can only become disabled by becoming too partisan, by becoming too little Pan-determined and so bringing himself into difficulties. These difficulties, however, are entirely the difficulties of consideration. As the thetan *considers,* so he *is.*

In the final analysis, the thetan has no problems of his own. The problems are always "other people's problems" and must exist in the mind, or the body, or in other people, or his surroundings, for *him* to have problems. Thus his difficulties are, in the main, the difficulties of staying in the game and keeping the game going.

If a thetan can suffer from anything, it is being *out-created* (created against too thoroughly). The manifestations of being out-created would be the destruction of his own creations and the overpowering presence of other creations. Thus, a thetan can be brought to believe that he is trapped if he is out-created.

In past dissertations on the subject of the mind and philosophies of life, there was a great deal of speculation and very little actual proof. Therefore, these philosophies were creations and one philosopher was at work out-creating another philosopher.

In Scientology, we have this single difference: We are dealing with *discoveries*.

The only things created about Scientology are the actual books and works in which Scientology is presented. The phenomena of Scientology are discovered and are held in common by all men and all life forms. There is no effort in Scientology to out-create each and every thetan that comes along. It is, of course, possible to conceive Scientology as a creation and to conceive that it is overwhelming. It should be viewed otherwise. For it is intended as an assistance to life at large, to enable life to make a better civilization and a better game.

"Scientology...is intended as an assistance
to life at large, to enable life to make
a better civilization and a better game."

CAUSATION AND KNOWLEDGE

Chapter Eight

CAUSATION AND KNOWLEDGE

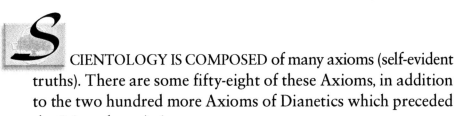CIENTOLOGY IS COMPOSED of many axioms (self-evident truths). There are some fifty-eight of these Axioms, in addition to the two hundred more Axioms of Dianetics which preceded the Scientology Axioms.

The first ten Axioms of Scientology are:

AXIOM 1   *Life is basically a Static.*

Definition: A Life Static has no mass, no motion, no wavelength, no location in space or in time. It has the ability to postulate and perceive.

Definition: In Scientology, the word "postulate" means to cause a thinkingness or consideration. It is a specially applied word and is defined as "causative thinkingness."

AXIOM 2   *The Static is capable of considerations, postulates and opinions.*

AXIOM 3   *Space, energy, objects, form and time are the result of considerations made and/or agreed upon or not by the Static, and are perceived solely because the Static considers that it can perceive them.*

AXIOM 4   *Space is a viewpoint of dimension.*

(Space is caused by looking out from a point. The only actuality of space is the agreed-upon consideration that one perceives through something and this we call space.)

AXIOM 5   *Energy consists of postulated particles in space.*

(One considers that energy exists and that he can perceive energy. One also considers that energy behaves according to certain agreed-upon laws. These assumptions or considerations are the totality of energy.)

AXIOM 6   *Objects consist of grouped particles and also of solid masses.*

AXIOM 7   *Time is basically a postulate that space and particles will persist.*

(The rate of their persistence is what we measure with clocks and the motion of heavenly bodies.)

AXIOM 8   *The apparency of time is the change of position of particles in space.*

AXIOM 9   *Change is the primary manifestation of time.*

AXIOM 10   *The highest purpose in this universe is the creation of an effect.*

These first ten Axioms of Scientology are the most fundamental "truths" (by which we mean "commonly held considerations").

Here we have thought and life and the physical universe in their relation, one to the other. Regardless of further considerations, ideas, assumptions and conditions, there lie beneath them these first ten truths.

It is as though one had entered into an honorable bargain with fellow beings to hold these things in common. Once this is done, or once such a "contract" or agreement exists, one has the fundamentals of a universe. Specialized considerations, based on the above Axioms, make one or another kind of universe. The physical universe, which we see around us and in which we live, was created on these fundamentals without regard to Who created it. Its creation was agreed upon. In order to perceive it, one must agree that it exists.

There are three classes of UNIVERSES:

1. There is first, foremost and most evident, the *physical universe* of spaces, stars, suns, land, sea, air and living forms.

2. Then there is the *other fellow's universe,* which may or may not be agreed upon by his associates. This he holds to himself. The phenomenon of this universe is included in the field of the mind, as described earlier.

3. Then listed last here, but first perceived, is *one's own universe.*

The phenomenon of universes is an interesting one, since one's own universe can be overwhelmed by the universes of others. These, in Scientology, we call *valences* (extra personalities, selves, apparent beingnesses). Valences and universes are the same thing, essentially.

For example, one while living in the physical universe can be overpowered by the universe of, let us say, father. While one still retains his own valence or identity, one is yet acting or thinking or suffering or feeling somewhat like father. Even though one is by oneself, there is this additional apparent beingness.

Although father is absent, his commands are still present. Thus we get such things as "duty," "obedience," "training" and even "education." Each one of these is caused by some part of another universe, to a greater or lesser degree.

Regardless of how one reacts to universes, he still remains, in some degree, himself. It is the effort of many to struggle against universes or valences. In fact, this is a game and the essence of games. The totality of the impulse of aberrated people is the effort to separate one's own self, as a thetan, from the various universes with which he feels himself too intimately associated. One is only oppressed by a universe when he feels he can have nothing of that universe. One is only victimized by "father's universe" when one is in protest against father. One protests against the physical universe only when he feels that he can have no part of it or does not belong in it or, as in religion, is not looked upon kindly by what he conceives to be the Creator of the physical universe.

There is a basic law about universes:

The postulates of the creator of any universe are the postulates which "work" in that universe.

Thus one may feel uncomfortable in the universe of another.

Universes (as considered in *games,* earlier) could be considered the "playing fields of life." One plays willingly or one plays unwillingly. When one begins to play unwillingly, he is apt to discover himself victimized by and interiorized into the universe of some game. It is against this phenomenon that a person protests.

Consider the matter of a jail. On the surface of it, as Voltaire discovered, a jail provides food and shelter and leisure time. This would seem to be the ambition of many people. But the jail provides, as well, a restriction without one's consent. The only difference between being in jail and being the king in a castle, so far as liberty is concerned, is one's own desires in the matter and one's own ability to command his environment:

As a king in a castle, one would be causative. His will, statement, thinkingness would have an effect upon others.

Being in a jail, one is an effect in that the thinkingness of others finds him its target.

Here we have, in terms of universes, the most rudimentary example of *cause* and *effect*.

We must, however, assume (because it is so evident) that an individual only gets into traps and circumstances he intends to get into. Certain it is that having gotten into such a position, he may be unwilling to remain in it. But a trap is always preceded by one's own choice of entrance. We must assume a very wide freedom of choice on the part of a thetan, since it is almost impossible to conceive how a thetan could get himself trapped even though he consented to it. By actual demonstration, a thetan goes through walls, barriers, vanishes space, appears anywhere at will and does other remarkable things. It must be, then, that an individual can be trapped only when he considers that he is trapped. In view of the fact that the totality of existence is based upon his own considerations, we find that the limitations he has must have been invited to himself. Otherwise, they could not be eradicated by the individual under processing, since the only one that is present with the preclear is the auditor and past associates of the preclear, while not present, do desensitize under processing in the preclear's mind. Therefore it must have been the preclear who kept them there. The preclear, by processing, can resolve all of his difficulties without going and finding other persons or consulting other universes.

Thus the totality of entrapment, aberration, even injury, torture, insanity and other distasteful items are basically considerations a thetan is making and holding right now, in present time. This must be the case, since time itself is a postulate or consideration on his own part.

The greatest philosophical clamor, or quarrel, has been waged around the subject of "knowledge" and there is nothing preposterous on the subject of knowledge that cannot be found in the philosophical texts. The superiority and ascendancy of Scientology depends upon the fact that it has transcended this philosophical quarrel on the subject of knowingness.

Scientology contains, in itself, the basics of KNOWLEDGE.

By knowledge we mean "assured belief, that which is known, information, instruction, enlightenment, learning, practical skill." By knowledge we mean "data, factors and whatever can be thought about or perceived."

The reason why knowledge has been misunderstood in philosophy is that it is only half the answer. There is no "allness" to knowledge. By definition, knowledge is "that which is perceived or learned or taken from another source." This patently means, then, that when one learns he is being an *effect*.

We see in Axiom 10 that:

The highest purpose in this universe is the creation of an effect.

This is in direct contradiction to knowledge (although one, of course, can know how to create an effect).

Opposed to knowledge, we have the neglected half of existence which is the *creation* of knowledge, the *creation* of data, the *creation* of thought, the *causative* consideration, self-evolved ideas as opposed to ideas otherwise evolved.

The reason Scientology is such a fascinating study is that it takes apart the other fellow's ideas and permits one to create some of his own. Scientology gives us the common denominators of objects, energies, spaces, universes, livingness and thought itself.

There is CAUSE and EFFECT.

Cause could be defined as "emanation." It could be defined also, for purposes of communication, as "source-point."

If you consider a river flowing to the sea, the place where it began would be the source-point or cause. And the place where it went into the sea would be the effect-point. And the sea would be the effect of the river. The man firing the gun is cause. The man receiving the bullet is effect. The one making a statement is causing the communication. The one receiving the statement is the effect of the communication. (A basic definition of communication is "cause-distance-effect.")

Almost all anxieties and upsets in human relations come about through an imbalance of cause and effect.

One must be willing, at once, to cause new data, statements, assumptions, considerations, and to receive ideas, assumptions, considerations.

So great is the anxiety of a thetan to cause an effect that he closely approaches those things which can cause an effect upon him. Thus a thetan becomes trapped.

On the face of it, so few thetans make causative data and so many receive data that it would seem, in view of the fact that a thetan can be touched only by his own consideration, that thetans are more anxious for effects than to be cause. However, this is not true in practice. In a game, one seeks to cause an effect and to receive no-effect.

It is learned, under close experiment, that there is nothing a thetan actually disdains on an effect level. He pretends not to like or enjoy certain effects and protests against them. But he knows very well that the mechanism of protest causes the effect to approach more closely (as a general rule). This came about by his repeated failure in games. Insisting on no-effect for himself, he lost. Then he had to say he liked the effect.

The prevailing anxiety, then, is to be an effect, not to be a cause. The entire subject of "responsibility" is a study of cause and effect, in that a person who wants no responsibility is anxious to be an effect only and a person who can assume responsibility must also be willing to be causative.

A thetan can be swung into a "state of consideration" by observing that it is commonly held by others. This keeps him in the universe and this keeps him being effect.

Study, investigation, receiving education and similar activity are all effect activities and result in the assumption of less responsibility. Thus, while it is true that a thetan cannot actually get into trouble, he can, by agreeing with the current agreed-upon thought in the universe where he finds himself, take a pattern of thinkingness which makes him less effective because he wishes to be an effect. If he feels he must gather all of his data from elsewhere, he is then the effect of knowledge, the effect of universes and postulates, and he tends to reduce his own ability to form or make knowledge.

In Scientology, we can communicate in full these circumstances since we are only calling to attention the pattern which an individual already, himself, holds. Thus we are not actually teaching him anything. We are only pointing out things he has already agreed with or himself caused.

It is only generally true that an individual is responsible for everything that happens to him. When an individual, wishing to cause many interesting effects, chooses to go into many universes or traps, he can become confused about what he is doing, where he is or what it is all about. Scientology points out that this can be seen or changed from a person's own viewpoint to bring about a change in his own condition.

As an example, a thetan has come to "believe" that the right way to get along in life is to do just as father did. This is an invitation to being in father's universe. Later on he changes his mind about this.

But he finds himself still in father's universe and doesn't like it. He would be more effective, more capable, if he were not now in father's universe. Customarily, in these unenlightened times, he waits for death to separate himself from the environment in which he finds himself and puts up with it until then. It is not necessary to do this now that we have Scientology. He can at any moment, given the proper steerage, vacate any trap in which he finds himself and begin again on a new series of considerations.

We cannot then talk about knowledge as a totality. It is a single datum. The "thirst for knowledge" would be the thirst for other thetans' postulates and would lead one to forget that he himself has been a party to the making of these postulates and that he himself had to follow a certain course in order to put himself in reach of other thetans' postulates.

Because one is the effect of knowledge, the causing of data, considerations or "facts" to come into existence separates one in distance from being an effect. If one is very anxious to be an effect, if this is his basic consideration, he will not take well to causing information to come into existence. But in order to get him out of the traps in which he finds himself, it is necessary to some degree that he does so.

Causing few barriers or traps, the individual then loses control over barriers or traps. Wishing to be an effect, of course he does lose control of barriers and traps. Otherwise, he cannot be entrapped by them. The thing to do to free him from a trap is to find what parts of the trap he himself is willing to *create, own, have* or *possess*. This places the barriers (which can be spaces, energy movements or obstacles) under his control. And his postulating that he can have or possess this or that, causes him to be willing to *be* or *occupy* the trap. The moment this occurs, he is no longer in the trap. Or even if he is still in it, to some degree he does not object to it and can leave it when he wishes.

CIVILIZATION AND SAVAGERY

The way to paralyze a nation entirely, and to make it completely ungovernable, would be to forbid education of any kind within its borders and to inculcate into every person within it the feeling that they must not receive any information from anybody about anything. To make a nation governable, it is necessary to hold a kindly view of education and to honor educative persons and measures. To conquer a land, it is not necessarily efficient to overwhelm them with guns. Once this is done, it is necessary to apply educative measures in order to bring about some sort of agreement amongst the people themselves, as well as between the conqueror and the subdued. Only in this way could one have a society, a civilization or, as we say in Scientology, a smoothly running game.

In other words, two extremes could be reached, neither one of which is desirable by the individual.

The first extreme could be reached by emphasis only upon self-created data or information. This would bring about not only a lack of interpersonal relations, but also an anxiety to have an effect which would, as it does in barbaric peoples, result in social cruelty unimaginable in a civilized nation. The other extreme would be to forbid in its entirety any self-created information and to condone only data or considerations generated by others than self. Here, we would create an individual with no responsibility, so easily handled that he would be only a puppet.

Self-created data is, then, not a bad thing. Neither is education. But one without the other, to hold it in some balance, will bring about a no-game condition or a no-civilization. Just as individuals can be seen by observing nations, so we see the primitive tribesman, with his complete contempt for truth and his emphasis on brutality and savagery for others, but not himself, is a no-civilization.

And we see at the other extreme China, slavishly dedicated to ancient scholars, incapable of generating within herself sufficient rulers to continue, without bloodshed, a nation.

We have noted the individual who must be the only one who can make a postulate or command, whose authority is dearer to him than the comfort or state of millions that have suffered from such men (Napoleon, Hitler, Kaiser Wilhelm, Frederick of Prussia, Genghis Khan, Attila). We have known, too, the scholar who has studied himself into blindness and is the world's greatest authority on government, or some such thing, who yet cannot himself manage his bank account or a dog with any certainty. Here we have, in either case, a total imbalance. The "world shaker" is himself unwilling to be any effect of any kind (and all the men named here were arrant personal cowards). And we have the opposite, a man who would not know what you were talking about if you told him to "get an idea of his own."

We see another example of this in the fundamental laws of warfare. A body of troops, to be effective, must be able to attack and to defend. Its implements must be divided 50 percent for attack and 50 percent for defense. In other words, even in a crude activity such as warfare, we find that no successful outcome is possible unless the troops can devote half of their energies to attack and half of them to defense.

In the much broader view of life, we discover on any dynamic that success, or a game, or activity, or life itself depends upon being willing to be cause as well as willing to be an effect. He who would give must be willing to receive. He who would receive must be willing to give. When these tenets are violated, the most fundamental principle of human relationships is violated. And the result is a no-game condition such as aberration, insanity, antisocialness, criminality, inactivity, laziness, tiredness, mania, fanaticism and all the other things against which men protest.

But imbalances between cause and effect also enter randomities into the game of life and cannot be neglected in their potential for creating a game.

Any information is valuable to the degree that you can use it. In other words, any information is valuable to the degree that you can make it yours. Scientology does not teach you. It only reminds you. For the information was yours in the first place. It is not only the science of life, but it is an account of what you were doing before you forgot what you were doing.

"Scientology does not teach you.
It only reminds you.
For the information was yours
in the first place."

Know and Not-Know

Chapter Nine

$\mathcal{K}$NOW AND NOT-KNOW

$\mathcal{I}$T IS A MECHANISM of thinkingness, whether one is postulating or receiving information, that one retains one's ability to know. It is equally important that one retains one's ability to not-know.

Thought consists entirely of KNOWING and NOT-KNOWING and the shades of gray between.

You will discover that most people are trying not to remember. In other words, they are trying to not-know. Education can only become burdensome when one is unable to not-know it. It is necessary that one be able to create, to receive, to know and to not-know information, data and thoughts. Lacking any one of these skills—for they are skills, no matter how native they are to the individual—one is apt to get into a chaos of thinkingness, or creatingness, or livingness.

You can look at any eccentric or aberrated person and discover rapidly, by an inspection of him, which one of these four factors he is violating. He either is unable to know or not-know his own created thoughts, or he is unable to know or not-know the thoughts of others. Somewhere, for some reason best known to him, in his anxiety to be part of the game, he has shelved (lost) one of these abilities.

Time is a process of knowing in the present and not-knowing in the future or the past.

Remembering is the process of knowing the past.

Prediction is the process of knowing the future.

Forgetting is the process of not-knowing the past.

And living "only for today" is the process of not-knowing the future.

Exercises in these various items rehabilitate not only the sanity or ability of the individual, but his general capability in living and playing the game.

"Thought consists entirely of
Knowing and Not-knowing
and the shades of gray between."

THE GOAL
OF SCIENTOLOGY

Chapter Ten

THE GOAL
OF SCIENTOLOGY

HE END OBJECT of Scientology is not the making into nothing of all of existence or the freeing of the individual of any and all traps everywhere.

The goal of Scientology is making the individual capable of living a better life in his own estimation and with his fellows and the playing of a better game.

Part Two

SCIENTOLOGY
PROCESSING

SCIENTOLOGY PROCESSING

SCIENTOLOGY PROCESSING

CIENTOLOGY IS APPLIED in many ways to many fields. One particular and specialized method of application of Scientology is its use on individuals and groups of people in addressing physical symptoms deriving from mental or spiritual factors and the improvement of their abilities and intelligence.

By PROCESSING is meant the "verbal exercising of a preclear in exact Scientology processes."

By PRECLEAR is meant "a person who is receiving processing."

There is a great deal of terminology and precision in these processes and their use, and they are not combinable with older mental activities, such as psychiatry, psychology, psychoanalysis, yoga, massage, etc.

However, these processes are capable of addressing the same ills of the mind as are delineated by older methodology, with the addition that Scientology is alone in its ability to successfully overcome those psychosomatic ills to which it is addressed. It is the only study known which is capable of producing marked and significant increases in intelligence and general ability.

Scientology processing, amongst other things, can improve the intelligence quotient of an individual, his ability or desire to communicate, his social attitudes, his capability and domestic harmony, his artistic creativity, his reaction time and his well-being.

An additional sphere of activity allied to processing is Preventive Scientology. In this branch of processing, an individual is inhibited or restrained from assuming states lower than he has already suffered from. In other words, the progress of tendencies, anxieties, habits and deteriorating activities can be halted or their occurrence can be prevented by Scientology. This is done by processing the individual on standard Scientology processes without particular attention to the disability involved.

A Scientology practitioner is called an AUDITOR ("one who listens, a listener").

Scientology processing is called AUDITING (by which the auditor "listens, computes and commands").

The auditor and the preclear are together out-of-doors, or in a quiet place where they will not be disturbed, or where they are not being subjected to interrupting influences.

The role of the auditor is to give the preclear certain and exact commands which the preclear can follow and perform.

The purpose of the auditor is to increase the ability of the preclear.

The Auditor's Code is the governing set of rules for the general activity of auditing. The code follows:

THE AUDITOR'S CODE

1 Do not evaluate for the preclear.

2 Do not invalidate or correct the preclear's data.

3 Use the processes which improve the preclear's case.

4 Keep all appointments once made.

5 Do not process a preclear after 10 P.M.

6 Do not process a preclear who is improperly fed.

7 Do not permit a frequent change of auditors.

8 Do not sympathize with the preclear.

9 Never permit the preclear to end the session on his own independent decision.

10 Never walk off from a preclear during a session.

11 Never get angry with a preclear.

12 Always reduce every communication lag encountered by continued use of the same question or process.

13 Always continue a process as long as it produces change and no longer.

14 Be willing to grant beingness to the preclear.

15 Never mix the processes of Scientology with those of various other practices.

16 Always remain in good two-way communication with the preclear during sessions.

The Auditor's Code governs the activity of the auditor during sessions (the time devoted to auditing). The activity of the Scientologist in general is governed by another broader code:

THE CODE OF A SCIENTOLOGIST

As a Scientologist, I pledge myself to the Code of Scientology for the good of all:

1 To hear or speak no word of disparagement to the press, public or preclears concerning any of my fellow Scientologists, our professional organization or those whose names are closely connected to this science.

2 To use the best I know of Scientology to the best of my ability to better my preclears, groups and the world.

3 To refuse to accept for processing and to refuse to accept money from any preclear or group I feel I cannot honestly help.

4 To deter to the fullest extent of my power anyone misusing or degrading Scientology to harmful ends.

5 To prevent the use of Scientology in advertisements of other products.

6 To discourage the abuse of Scientology in the press.

7 To employ Scientology to the greatest good of the greatest number of dynamics.

8 To render good processing, sound training and good discipline to those students or peoples entrusted to my care.

9 To refuse to impart the personal secrets of my preclears.

10 To engage in no unseemly disputes with the uninformed on the subject of my profession.

As it can be seen, both of these codes are designed to protect the preclear as well as Scientology and the auditor in general.

As these codes evolve from many years of observation and experience by a great number of people, it can be said that they are intensely important and are probably complete. Failure to observe them has resulted in a failure of Scientology. Scientology can do what it can do only when it is used within the limits of these two codes. Thus it can be seen that the interjection of peculiarities or practices by the auditor into Scientology processing, can actually nullify and eradicate the benefits of that processing.

Any hope or promise in Scientology is conditional upon its good use by the individual and its use, in particular, within the limits of these two codes.

BEINGNESS, DOINGNESS AND HAVINGNESS

Chapter Twelve

BEINGNESS, DOINGNESS AND HAVINGNESS

THE GAME OF LIFE demands that one assumes a *beingness* in order to accomplish a *doingness* in the direction of *havingness*. (Chapter Three, The Conditions of Existence.)

If you ask an auditor how these work in processing, he will tell you that there is a specialized form of each of these conditions.

BEINGNESS = IDENTITY

The processing form of BEINGNESS is IDENTITY.

To achieve a betterment of beingness and the granting of beingness, the auditor remedies with processing the scarcity of identities of the preclear. The preclear is often found in *valences* (other identities): his father's or mother's or marital partner's or any or all of thousands of possible people. He is unable to achieve or obtain (he thinks) enough identity or an identity of his own. He decries or criticizes the identities of others (fails to grant beingness to them).

He, himself, cannot obtain enough identity to feel he has an identity. Identity is so scarce that it's too valuable. Nobody must have one. To be with such a person is therefore an uncomfortable experience, since he does not credit our identity (does not grant us beingness).

The "cure" for this is elementary. Let us say he is obviously in father's valence (identity). He got into father's valence when he found he could get no attention from mother. Observing that father got some of her attention, he took father's identity. However, let us say he didn't like father. The auditor finds him hating "himself." "Himself" is really father.

A clever auditor would see that while he was in father's valence, it was really mother's attention that was sought (see later, Identities — Valences).

The auditor does not inform his preclear of such a finding. He asks the preclear to:

"Lie about (lowest form of creativity) *identities which would attract mother's attention."*

Then, when the preclear can do this, the auditor would have him:

"Invent identities which would attract mother's attention."

Suddenly the preclear would be no longer in father's valence. However, he would have been not only in father's but also in mother's valence, so the same process would have to be done on father:

"Lie about," the auditor would say, *"identities which would attract father's attention,"* then *"Invent"* one, until the preclear had many and would no longer be in mother's valence.

Solving father and mother valences is fundamental, since most people are somewhat "in them" or revolted from them. But people can be "stuck" in all sorts of identities, even bedposts when humans are too valuable to be used.

The rule is that the more a person is "stuck" in a valence or identity, the fewer he conceives to exist. And the harder he thinks it is to get attention. Thus he can become exhibitionistic (displaying himself too thoroughly, being too much *there* at all times) or he can become dispersed (hiding himself, being vague, *not there* most of the time).

People err, in identity, in being too apparent or too little apparent. The remedy of either is the remedy of their scarcity of identity.

IDENTITY AND ATTENTION

One "needs" an IDENTITY to play the game (as covered later, Game and No-Game Conditions) but mainly to "get" ATTENTION.

A being looks at things. To balance the flow of his attention, he feels he must also be looked at. Thus he becomes attention-hungry.

For instance, unlike races of Asia and Africa, the white does not usually believe he can get attention from matter or objects. The other cultures believe for the most part (and it is all a matter of consideration) that rocks, trees, walls, etc., can give them attention. The white race seldom believes this and so is likely to become anxious about people.

Thus the white saves people, prevents famine, flood, disease and revolution—for people, as the only purveyors of attention, are scarce.

The white goes further. He often believes he can get attention only from whites and that attention from other races is worthless. Thus the other cultures are not very progressive but, by and large, saner. And the white race is progressive but more frantic. The other cultures do not understand white concern for "bad conditions," since "what are a few million dead men?" There are plenty of identities and there is plenty of attention, they think. The white can't understand them. Nor can they understand the white.

Attention and Identity form a group of two. Attention makes space. Identity closes space.

Attention is a method of knowing. Inattention is a method of not-knowing.

Identity is a method of making known. Lack of Identity is a method of making unknown.

VALENCES

The whole study of VALENCES is a fascinating one.

A valence is defined as "a false identity assumed unwittingly." An identity is modified by valences. People who can be nobody may try to be everybody. People who are seeking a way out of scarcity of identity may become fixed in false valences. Nations can become fixed in valences of countries they have conquered in war, etc., etc.

A rule is that a person assumes the identity of that which gets attention. Another rule is that the person assumes the identity of that which makes him fail (for he gave it *his* attention, didn't he?).

There *is* a basic personality, a person's *own* identity. He colors or drowns this with valences as he loses or wins in life. He *can* be dug up.

IDENTITIES—VALENCES

There are four IDENTITIES or VALENCES.

Own Valence

When one is in his "own" valence, he is said to be "himself." As he departs from his own identity, he comes into the following:

Exchanged Valence

One has directly superimposed the identity of another on his own.

Example: Daughter becomes own mother to some degree.

Remedy: One directly runs out mother.

Attention Valence

One has become the valence B because one wants attention from C.

Example: One becomes mother because mother received attention from father while self did not.

Remedy: Run out father even though preclear appears in valence of mother.

Synthetic Valence

One takes a valence about which he has been told.

Example: Mother tells child false things about father, accuses child of being like father, with result that child is forced into father's valence.

Remedy: Run out mother even though preclear does not seem to be near mother's valence.

Do = Effect

DOING can be defined as the action of creating an EFFECT.

An effect in creation is action.

An auditor, processing a preclear, would always use "effect processes" to increase doingness.

"What effect could you create on father?" would be a typical auditor question.

If a preclear is fixated by books, a machine, a tool, a person, the auditor asks him to *"Lie about,"* then *"Invent,"* effects he could create upon it. At first, the preclear may be able to think of none.

Then, as the process is continued, he may become wildly imaginative or even cruel. Further running will bring the preclear into a more comfortable frame of mind. Criminals or maniacs are people who are frantically attempting to create an effect long after they know they cannot. They cannot then create decent effects, only violent effects. Neither can they work *(do)*.

Despair of creating an effect brings about aberration and irrational conduct. It also brings about laziness and carelessness.

Command of attention is necessary to creating an effect. Therefore when one conceives he cannot easily get attention, he seeks to create stronger effects. He creates effects to get attention. He gets attention to create effects.

As in Axiom 10:

The creation of an effect is the highest purpose in this universe.

Thus when one cannot create effects, he has no purpose. And thus it works out in life. It may be all right to be a stern and unrelenting superior or parent, but such create laziness and criminals. If one cannot have an effect created upon one (and one is known to another), very definitely harmful results will ensue.

As one believes he creates the *least* effect upon unconscious or dead people, these, as in hospitals or China, become the subject of much aberrated activity.

"What effect could you create on an unconscious person (or a *dead person)?"* asked over and over by an auditor obtains some astonishing results.

An artist stops his work when he believes he can no longer create an effect.

A person actually dies for lack of effect.

But security often depends on being able to create *no* effect.

The whole subject of survival is bound up in no-effect. Obviously those things on which no-effect can be made survive.

If one is anxious about survival (a foolish thing, for he can't do anything else), he becomes anxious to have about him things which resist all effects. But as his only anxiety is about the survival of a valence or identity, remedy of the scarcity of these can resolve the matter.

Another cycle-of-action, containing also the classes of effects, is START-CHANGE-and-STOP. This is the definition of CONTROL.

HAVINGNESS

As there must be a playing field for a game to be held (see later, Game and No-Game Conditions), so there must be HAVINGNESS.

One must be able to possess.

There are millions of methods of possession in life. The obvious one becomes overlooked. If one can see a thing he can have it – *if* he thinks he can.

The degree to which one can live is the degree to which one can own. To own is not to label or cart away. To own is to be able to see or touch or occupy.

One loses to the degree he is forbidden to have.

But to play a game, one must be able to believe he can't have.

EFFECT AND HAVE

EFFECT and HAVE form a pair like ATTENTION and IDENTITY.

An effect should be on or against something. Thus havingness. If one's attention never meets anything, he doesn't always like it. Thus he wants objects.

Effect makes distance. Have shortens distance.

PROBLEMS

Man or any life form in this universe seems to love PROBLEMS.

A problem is more important than freedom. Problems keep up interest.

When a man *has* a problem very thoroughly and can't solve it, he really has too few problems. He needs more.

The insanity amongst the idle is a matter of problem-scarcity.

A problem is defined as "two or more purposes in opposition." Or "intention-versus-intention."

Out of the conditions-of-existence can come many complex problems.

If a man had *all* the attention in the world, he would be unhappy. If he had *all* the identities possible, he would still be unhappy. If he could blow up Earth or create *any* other huge effect he wanted (without limit), he would be miserable (or insane). If he could own *everything* everywhere, he would be dulled to apathy. Or so it seems. For these conditions-of-existence are all subordinate to the need of problems by current Scientology reasoning and results.

Thus, to have a person *"Lie about problems"* or *"Invent problems"* of the same size as the ones he has or the valence he is in, or to *"Invent data"* of the same or different size as the one he is fixed upon, is to make a well man.

Probably the problem is the antidote to unconsciousness. It is certainly the antidote for boredom.

But in making up the problems of life, he consults the conditions-of-existence, *Be-Do-Have,* and their necessary partner in every case, *Attention.*

"Man or any life form
in this universe seems to love problems.
A problem is more important than freedom.
Problems keep up interest."

Chapter Thirteen

SELF-DETERMINISM
AND PAN-DETERMINISM

SELF-DETERMINISM AND PAN-DETERMINISM

SELF-DETERMINISM

SELF-DETERMINISM is a condition of determining the actions of self. It is a First (Self) Dynamic action and leaves the remaining seven undetermined or, in actuality, in opposition to the self.

Thus, if one wants to take on the rest of life in a free-for-all fight, one could be entirely insistent upon total Self-determinism. As the remainder of the dynamics must have a say in one's self to function, they fight at once any attempt at total Self-determinism.

PAN-DETERMINISM

PAN-DETERMINISM means determining the action of self and others. It means wider determinism than self.

In an aberrated fashion we see this in an effort to control all others to aggrandize (make important) self. Pan-determinism is *across* determinism or determinism of two sides. If one controls (monitors) both sides of a chess game, one is "above" the game.

One is Self-determined, then, in any situation in which he is *fighting*.

He is Pan-determined in any situation which he is *controlling*.

To become Pan-determined, rather than only Self-determined, it is necessary to view both sides.

A problem is an intention-versus-intention. It is then something that has two opposing sides. By creating problems, one tends to view both sides in opposition and so becomes Pan-determined.

Thus a problem only *appears* to be necessary to Man. The problem is the closest reality Man has to Pan-determinism. In processing, the invention of problems then shows a wider view and so exteriorizes one from difficulty.

"Pan-determinism is across determinism
or determinism of two sides."

$\mathcal{G}$AME AND
NO-GAME CONDITIONS

GAME AND NO-GAME CONDITIONS

N SCIENTOLOGY, the most important single elements to the auditor are GAME CONDITIONS and NO-GAME CONDITIONS.

REASON

Reason: All *games* are aberrative.

All processing is directed toward establishing game conditions.

Little or no processing is directed toward no-game conditions.

Therefore it is of the utmost importance to know exactly what these are, for one could be superficial about it and lose.

RULE

Rule: All *games* are aberrative; some are fun.

ᵉLEMENTS OF GAMES

The ELEMENTS OF GAMES to the auditor are:

A game consists of freedoms, barriers and purposes.

In a game, one's own team or self must receive no-effect and must deliver an effect upon the other team or opponent.

A game should have space and, preferably, a playing field.

A game is played in the same time continuum for both sides (all players).

A game must have something which one does not have in order for it to be won.

Some part of the dynamics must be excluded for a game condition to exist. The amount of the dynamics excluded represents the tone of the game.

Games occur only when there is intention-opposing-intention, purpose-opposing-purpose.

A scarcity of games forces the preclear to accept less desirable games.

Participation in any game (whether it be the game of "sick man," "jealous wife" or "polo") is preferable to being in a no-game condition.

The type of game entered by a person is determined by his consideration as to how much and what kind of an effect he may receive while trying to deliver an effect.

Games are the basic mechanism for continuing attention.

To play a game, one must be able to not-know his past and future and not-know his opponent's complete intentions.

GAME CONDITIONS

GAME CONDITIONS are:

Attention

Identity

Effect on opponents

No-effect on self

Can't have on opponents and goals and their areas

Have on self, tools of play, own goals and field

Purpose

Problems of play

Self-determinism

Opponents

The possibility of loss

The possibility of winning

Communication

Non-arrival

Control

NO-GAME CONDITIONS

NO-GAME CONDITIONS are:

Knowing all

Not-knowing everything

Serenity

Namelessness

No-effect on opponent

Effect on self or team

Others have everything

Self can't have

Solutions

Pan-determinism

Friendship with all

Understanding

Total communication

No communication of any kind whatsoever

Win

Lose

No universe

No playing field

Arrival

Death

Process *only* with those conditions listed as Game Conditions. Do not process directly toward those conditions listed as No-Game Conditions. So doing, the auditor will run out (erase) the aberrative effect of games and restore an ability to play a game.

"A game consists of
freedoms, barriers and purposes."

*A*UDITING:
PROCEDURES AND
PROCESSES

AUDITING: PROCEDURES AND PROCESSES

THE CONDITIONS OF AUDITING

CERTAIN DEFINITE CONDITIONS must prevail and a certain methodology must be followed in order that processing may be beneficial to its fullest extent.

Probably the first condition is a good grasp of Scientology and its mission in the world.

The second condition would be a relaxed state of mind on the part of the auditor and the confidence that his use of Scientology upon the preclear will not produce a harmful result.

The third requisite should be finding a preclear. By this it is literally meant that one should discover somebody willing to be processed. And having discovered one so willing, should then make sure that he is aware that he is there being processed.

The fourth requisite would be a quiet place in which to audit with every precaution taken that the preclear will not be interrupted or burst in upon or unduly startled during processing.

ᴀ AUDITING PROCEDURES

All requisites for auditing from here on are entirely concerned with PROCEDURES and PROCESSES.

By auditing procedure is meant "the general model of how one goes about addressing a preclear."

This includes an ability to place one question, worded exactly the same way over and over again, to the preclear – no matter how many times the preclear has answered the question.

It should include the ability to acknowledge with a *"good"* and *"all right"* every time a preclear executes or completes the execution of a command. It should include the ability to accept a communication from the preclear. When the preclear has something to say, the auditor should pay some attention to the communication and should acknowledge the fact that he has received the preclear's communication.

Procedure also includes the ability to sense when the preclear is being overstrained by processing, or is being unduly annoyed, and to handle such crises in the session to prevent the preclear from leaving.

An auditor should have the ability of handling startling remarks or occurrences by the preclear. An auditor should also have the knack of preventing the preclear from talking obsessively, since prolonged conversation markedly reduces the havingness of the preclear. The sooner long dissertations by the preclear are cut off, the better for the session (the period of time devoted to auditing) in general.

Processes, as distinct from procedures, consist of utilizing the principle of the "gradient scale" to the end of placing the preclear in better control of himself, his mind, the people and the universe around him.

By gradient scale is meant "a proceeding from simplicity toward greater difficulty," giving the preclear always no more than he can do, but giving him as much as he can do until he can handle a great deal.

The idea here is to give the preclear nothing but wins and to refrain from giving the preclear losses in the game of processing. Thus it can be seen that processing is a team activity and is not itself a game, whereby the auditor opposes and seeks to defeat the preclear and the preclear seeks to defeat the auditor. For when this condition exists, little results in processing.

Exact Processes

The earliest stage of auditing consists in taking over control of the preclear, so as to restore to the preclear more control of himself than he has had. The most fundamental step is, then, *location*—whereby the preclear is made to be aware of the fact that he is in an auditing room, that an auditor is present and that the preclear is being a preclear. Those conditions will become quite apparent if one realizes that it would be very difficult for a son to process a father. A father is not likely to recognize, in his auditor, anything else than the boy he raised. Therefore, the father would have to be made aware of the fact that the son was a competent practitioner before the father could be placed under control in processing.

Look at Me; Who Am I?

One of the most elementary commands in Scientology is:

"Look at me; who am I?"

After a preclear has been asked to do this many times, until he can do so quickly and accurately and without protest, it can be said that the preclear will have "found" the auditor.

Start-Change-and-Stop

The preclear is asked by the auditor to control — which is to say, *start, change* and *stop* (the anatomy of control) anything he is capable of controlling.

In a very bad case, this might be a very small object being pushed around on a table, being started and changed and stopped each time, specifically and only at the auditor's command, until the preclear *realizes that he, himself, can start, change and stop the object:*

"When I say start, you start the (object) *in that direction* (auditor indicates direction). *Okay?"*

"Start."

When the preclear has:

"Did you start the (object)?*"*

"When I say change, you change the (object's) *position from* (location designated by auditor) *to* (location designated by auditor). *Okay?"*

"Change."

When the preclear has:

"Did you change the (object)?*"*

"I am going to tell you to get the (object) *moving in that direction* (auditor indicates direction). *When I say stop, you stop the* (object). *Okay?"*

"Get the (object) *moving."*

"Stop."

When the preclear has:

"Did you stop the (object)?*"*

In all of his commands, the auditor must be careful never to give a second command before the first one has been fully obeyed.

Sometimes four or five hours spent in this exercise are very well spent on a very difficult preclear.

The preclear is then asked to start, change and stop his own body, under the auditor's specific and precise direction.

The auditor substitutes *"body"* in place of "(object)" in the above commands.

A preclear in this procedure is walked around the room and is made to *start, change* the direction of and *stop* his body, one of these at a time, in emphasis, until *he realizes that he can do so with ease.*

Only now could it be said that a session is well in progress or that a preclear is securely under the auditor's command.

It should be noted, especially, that the goal of Scientology is better self-determinism for the preclear. This rules out, at once, hypnotism, drugs, alcohol or other control mechanisms used by other and older therapies. It will be found that such things are not only not necessary, but they are in direct opposition to the goals of greater ability for the preclear.

The principal points of concentration for the auditor now become:

1. The ability of the preclear to *have.*

2. The ability of the preclear to *not-know.*

3. And the ability of the preclear to *play a game.*

An additional factor is the ability of the preclear to *be himself* and not a number of other people, such as his father, his mother, his marital partner or his children (see earlier, Beingness, Doingness and Havingness).

Have (Trio)

The ability of the preclear is increased by addressing *havingness* with the process known as the *Trio*. These are three questions or, rather, commands:

1. *"Look around here and tell me what you could have."*

2. *"Look around here and tell me what you would permit to remain in place."*

3. *"Look around and tell me with what you could dispense."*

No. 1 above is used usually about ten times, then No. 2 is used five times and No. 3 is used once. This ratio of ten, five and one would be an ordinary or routine approach to havingness. The end in view is to bring the preclear into a condition whereby *he can possess or own or have whatever he sees, without further conditions, ramifications or restrictions.*

This is the most therapeutic of all processes, elementary as it might seem. It is done without too much two-way communication or discussion with the preclear. And it is done until the preclear can answer questions 1, 2 and 3 equally well.

It should be noted at once that twenty-five hours of use of this process by an auditor upon a preclear (over a period of several sessions) usually brings about a very high rise in tone. By saying twenty-five hours, it is intended to give the idea of the length of time the process should be used. As it is a strain on the usual person to repeat the same question over and over, it will be seen that an auditor should be well disciplined or very well trained before he audits.

In the case of a preclear who is very unable, *"can't have"* is substituted for *"have"* in the first question above, for a few hours, until the preclear is ready for the Trio in its *"have"* form.

Selecting categories (which are the eight dynamics) and selecting them as they seem to be put forward by the preclear, one asks what these categories *"can't have."* One does *not* stress what the individual himself *"can't have,"* for to do so would make the individual postulate against himself. Let us suppose that the preclear is a man and that the category "women" had been chosen. The auditing question would then be:

"Look around here and tell me what women can't have."

On the male preclear, of course:

"Look around here and tell me what men can't have" would also be runnable, since the truth of the matter is the preclear is not a male, but has a male body.

On other categories, the question is the same:

"Look around here and tell me what (category) *can't have."*

(This "can-can't" is the plus and minus aspect of all thought and in Scientology is called by a specialized word — *dichotomy.)*

Not-Know

The rehabilitation of the ability of the preclear to *not-know* is also rehabilitation of the preclear in the time stream, since the process of time consists of *knowing* the *present* moment and *not-knowing* the *past* and *not-knowing* the *future* — simultaneously.

This process, like all other Scientology processes, is repetitive. The process is run, ordinarily, only after the preclear is in very good condition and is generally run in an exterior, well-inhabited place.

Here the auditor, without exciting public comment, indicates a person and asks the preclear:

"Can you not-know something about that person?"

The auditor does not permit the preclear to not-know things which the preclear already doesn't know. The preclear not-knows only those things which are visible and apparent about the person.

This is also run on other objects in the environment, such as walls, floors, chairs and other things. The auditor should not be startled when, for the preclear, large chunks of the environment start to disappear. This is ordinary routine and, in effect, the preclear should make the entirety of the environment disappear at his own command. The environment does not disappear for the auditor. The end goal of this Not-Know process is *the disappearance of the entire universe, under the preclear's control* (but only for the preclear).

It will be discovered while running this that the preclear's havingness may deteriorate. If this happens, he was not run enough on the Trio before he was run on this process. It is only necessary in such a case to intersperse *"Look around here and tell me what you could have,"* with the Not-Know command, to keep the preclear in good condition.

Drop of havingness is manifested by nervous agitation, obsessive talk, or semi-unconsciousness or dopiness on the part of the preclear. These manifestations only indicate reduction of havingness.

The reverse of the question here is:

"Tell me something that you would be willing to have that person (indicated by the auditor) *not-know about you."*

Both sides of the question have to be run (audited). This process can be continued for twenty-five hours (or even fifty or seventy-five hours) of auditing, with considerable benefit, so long as it does not react too violently upon the preclear in terms of loss of havingness.

It should be noted, in running either the Trio or Not-Know on a preclear, that the preclear may *exteriorize.*

In other words, it may become apparent (either by his observation or that the preclear informs him) that the auditor has exteriorized a preclear. In Chapter Seven, The Parts of Man, there is an explanation of this phenomenon. In modern auditing, the auditor does not do anything odd about this beyond receive and be interested in the preclear's statement of the fact. The preclear should not be permitted to become alarmed, since it is a usual manifestation. A preclear is in better condition and will audit better exteriorized than "in his head."

An actual ability to not-know is an ability to erase the *past* by self-command, without suppressing it with energy or going into any other method, and is necessary to help the preclear. It is the primary rehabilitation in terms of knowingness. Forgetting is a lower manifestation than not-knowingness.

Play a Game

The third ability to be addressed by the auditor is the ability of the preclear to *play a game*.

First and foremost in the requisites to play a game is the ability to control. One must be able to control something in order to participate in a game. Therefore, the general rehabilitation of control (by starting, changing and stopping things) is a rehabilitation in the ability to play a game.

When a preclear refuses to recover, it is because the preclear is using his "state" as a game and does not believe that there is any better game for him to play than the state he is in. He may protest if this is called a "game."

Nevertheless, any condition will surrender if the auditor has the preclear *"Invent"* similar conditions or even *"Tell lies"* about the existing condition. Inventing *games* or inventing *conditions* or inventing *problems,* alike, rehabilitate the ability to play a game.

Chief amongst these various rehabilitation factors are *control* (start, change and stop), *problems* and the *willingness to overwhelm* or *be overwhelmed*. One ceases to be able to have games when one loses control over various things, when one becomes short of problems and when one is unwilling to be overwhelmed (in other words, to lose) or to overwhelm (to win).

It will be found while running havingness (as in the Trio above) that one may run down the ability to play a game, since havingness is in part the reward of a game.

In the matter of *problems,* it will be seen that these are completely necessary to the playing of a game. The anatomy of a problem is intention-versus-intention. This is, in essence, the purpose of all games — to have two sides, each one with an opposed intention. (Technically, a problem is two or more *purposes* in conflict.) It is very simple to detect whether or not the preclear is suffering from a scarcity of games. The preclear who needs more games clutches to himself various present time problems. If an auditor is confronted with a preclear who is being obsessed by a problem in present time, he knows two things:

1. That the preclear's ability to play a game is low.

2. That he must run an exact process at once to rehabilitate the preclear in session.

It often happens at the beginning of an auditing session that the preclear has encountered a heavy present time problem between sessions. The preclear must always be consulted, before the session is actually in progress, as to whether or not he has anything worrying him.

To a preclear who is worried about some present time situation or problem, no other process has any greater effectiveness than the following one.

Problems of Comparable Magnitude

The auditor, with a very *brief* discussion of the problem, asks the preclear to:

"Invent a problem of comparable magnitude."

He may have to reword this request to make the preclear understand it completely. But the auditor wants, in essence, the preclear to *invent* or *create* a problem he considers similar to the problem he has.

If the preclear is unable to do this, it is necessary then to have him *"Lie about"* the problem which he has. Lying is the lowest order of creativeness. After he has lied about the problem for a short time, it will be found that he will be able to invent problems. He should be made to invent problem after problem, until *he is no longer concerned with his present time problem.*

The auditor should understand that a preclear who is now "willing to do something about the problem" has not been run long enough on the *"Invent a problem of comparable magnitude."* As long as the preclear is attempting to *do* something about the problem, the problem is still of obsessive importance to him. No session can be continued successfully until such a present time problem is entirely "flat." And it has been the experience that when a present time problem was not completely eradicated by this process, the remainder of the session or, indeed, the entire course of auditing may be interrupted.

When a preclear does not seem to be advancing under auditing, a thing which he does markedly and observedly, it must then be supposed that the preclear has a present time problem which has not been eradicated and which must be handled in auditing. Although the auditor gives the preclear to understand that he, too, believes this present time problem is extremely important, the auditor should not *believe* that this process will not handle any present time problem—since it will.

This process should be done on some preclears in company with the Trio.

If the preclear is asked to *"Lie about"* or *"Invent a problem of comparable magnitude"* and while doing so becomes agitated or unconscious or begins to talk wildly or obsessively, it must be assumed that he will have to have some havingness run on him, until the agitation or manifestation ceases, so that the Problems of Comparable Magnitude process can be resumed.

Overwhelming

Another aspect of the ability to play a game is the *willingness to win* and the *willingness to lose*. An individual has to be willing to be *cause* or willing to be an *effect*. As far as games are concerned, this is reduced to a willingness to win and a willingness to lose. People become afraid of defeat and afraid of failure. The entire anatomy of failure is only that one's postulates or intentions are reversed in action. For instance, one intends to strike a wall and strikes it. That is a win. One intends not to strike a wall and doesn't strike it. That is again a win. One intends not to strike a wall and strikes it. That is a lose. One intends to strike a wall and can't strike it. This is again a lose. It will be seen in this, as well as other things, that the most significant therapy there is, is *changing the mind.* All things are as one *considers* they are and in *no* other way. If it is sufficiently simple to give the definition of winning and losing, so it is simple to process the matter.

This condition is best expressed in processing by a process known as *Overwhelming*.

An elementary way of running this is to take the preclear outside where there are numbers of people to observe and, indicating a person, ask the preclear:

"What could overwhelm that person?"

When the preclear answers this, he is asked about the same person:

"What could that person overwhelm?"

He is then asked, as the third question:

"Look around here and tell me what you could have."

These three questions are run one after the other.

Then another person is chosen and then the three questions are asked again. This process can be varied in its wording, but the central idea must remain as above. The preclear can be asked:

"What would you permit to overwhelm that person?"

And:

"What would you permit that person to overwhelm?"

And, of course:

"Look around here and tell me what you could have."

This is only one of a number of possible processes on the subject of overwhelming. But it should be noted that asking the preclear to think of things which would overwhelm *him* could be fatal to the case. Where overwhelming is handled, the preclear should be given a detached view.

Separateness

As a counterposition to havingness processes (Trio), but one which is less therapeutic, is *Separateness*. One asks the preclear to:

"Look around and discover things which are separate from you."

This is repeated over and over. It is, however, destructive of havingness even though it will occasionally prove beneficial.

*U*SE OF PROCESSES

It will be seen that *havingness* (barriers), *not-knowingness* (being in present time and not in the past or the future), *purposes* (problems, antagonists or intention-versus-intention) and *separateness* (freedom) well cover the anatomy of games.

It is not to be thought, however, that havingness addresses itself only to games. Many other factors enter into it. In amongst all of these, it *is* of the greatest single importance.

In these days of Scientology, one addresses the subjective self (the mind) as little as possible. One keeps the preclear alert to the broad environment around him. An address to the various energy patterns of the mind is less beneficial than exercises which directly approach other people or the physical universe. Therefore, asking a preclear to sit still and answer the question *"What could you have?"* (when it is answered by the preclear from his experience or on the "score of things" which are not present) is found to be nontherapeutic and is found, instead, to decrease the ability and intelligence of the preclear. This is what is known as a "subjective (inside the mind only) process."

These are the principal processes which produce marked gains. There are other processes and there are combinations of processes, but these given here are the most important. A Scientologist, knowing the mind completely, can of course do many "tricks" with the conditions of people to improve them. One of these is the ability to address a psychosomatic illness, such as a crippled leg which, having nothing physically wrong with it, is yet not usable.

The auditor could ask the preclear:

"Tell me a lie about your leg," with a possible relief of the pain or symptoms.

Asking the preclear repeatedly:

"Look around here and tell me something your leg could have," would undoubtedly release the somatic.

Asking the preclear with the bad leg:

"What problem could your leg be to you?"

Or requiring him to:

"Invent a problem of comparable magnitude to your leg," would produce a distinct change in the condition of the leg.

This would apply to any other body part or organ.

It would also apply, strangely enough, to the preclear's possessions. If a preclear had a vehicle or cart which was out of repair or troublesome to him, one could ask him:

"What problem could a cart be to you?"

Requesting him to:

"Invent (many such problems)," one would discover that he had solved his problems with the cart.

There is the phenomenon in existence that the preclear already has many set games. When one asks him to give the auditor problems, he already has the manifestations of *As-ising* (or erasing) taking place. Thought erases. Therefore, the number of problems or games the preclear could have would be reduced by asking him to recount those which he already has. Asking the preclear to recount or describe his symptoms is far *less* than therapeutic and may result in a worsening of those symptoms (contrary to what some schools of thought have believed in the past, but which accounts for their failures).

ᴀ*A*UDITING: THINGS TO AVOID

There are specific things which one must avoid in auditing. These follow:

1. SIGNIFICANCES. The easiest thing a thetan does is change his mind. The most difficult thing he does is handle the environment in which he finds himself situated. Therefore, asking a thetan to run out various ideas is a fallacy. It is a mistake. Asking the preclear to think over something can also be an error. Asking a preclear to do exercises which concern his mind alone can be entirely fatal. A preclear is processed between himself and his environment. If he is processed between himself and his mind, he is processed up "too short a view" and his condition will worsen.

2. TWO-WAY COMMUNICATION. There can be far too much two-way communication or far too much communication in an auditing session. Communication involves the reduction of havingness. Letting a preclear talk on and on, or obsessively, is to let a preclear reduce his havingness. The preclear who is permitted to go on talking will talk himself down Tone Scale and into a bad condition. It is better for the auditor simply and discourteously to tell a preclear to "shut up," than to have the preclear run himself "out of the bottom" on havingness.

You can observe this for yourself if you permit a person, who is not too able to talk about his troubles, to keep on talking. He will begin to talk more and more hectically. He is reducing his havingness. He will eventually talk himself down the Tone Scale into Apathy, at which time he will be willing to tell you (as you insist upon it) that he "feels better" when, as a matter of fact, he is actually worse.

Asking a preclear, "How do you feel now?" can reduce his havingness, since he looks over his present time condition and As-ises some mass.

3. TOO MANY PROCESSES. It is possible to run a preclear on too many processes in too short a time with a reduction of the preclear's recovery. This is handled by observing the "communication lag" of the preclear. It will be discovered that the preclear will space his answers, to a repeated question, differently with each answer. When a long period ensues between his answer to the question a second time, he is said to have a communication lag. The communication lag is "the length of time between the placing of the question by the auditor and the *answering of that exact question* by the preclear." It is not the length of time between the placing of the question by the auditor and *some statement* by the preclear. It will be found that the communication lag lengthens and shortens on a repeated question. The question, on the tenth time it has been asked, may detect no significant lag. This is the time to stop asking that question, since it now has no appreciable communication lag. One can leave any process when the communication lag for *three successive questions* is the same.

In order to get from one process to another, one employs a "communication bridge" which, to a marked degree, reduces the liability of too many processes. A communication bridge is always used. Before a question is asked, the preclear should have the question discussed with him and the wording of the question agreed upon as though he were making a contract with the auditor. The auditor says that he is going to have the preclear do certain things and finds out if it's "all right" with the preclear if the auditor asks him to do these things.

This is the first part of a communication bridge. It precedes all questions. But when one is changing from one process to another, the bridge becomes a bridge indeed. One "levels out" the old process by asking the preclear "whether or not he doesn't think it is safe to leave that process now?" One discusses the possible benefit of the process and then tells the preclear that he is no longer going to use that process. Now he tells the preclear he is going to use a new process, describes the process and gets an agreement on it. When the agreement is achieved, then he uses this process. The communication bridge is used at all times. The last half of it, the agreement on a new process, is always used before any process is begun.

4. FAILURE TO HANDLE THE PRESENT TIME PROBLEM. Probably more cases are stalled or found unable to benefit in processing because of the neglect of the present time problem (as covered above) than any other single item.

5. UNCONSCIOUSNESS, DOPINESS OR AGITATION on the part of the preclear is not a mark of good condition. It is a loss of havingness. The preclear must never be processed into unconsciousness or dopiness. He should always be kept alert. The basic phenomenon of unconsciousness is "a flow which has flowed too long in one direction." If one talks too long at somebody, he will render him unconscious. In order to wake up the target of all that talk, it is necessary to get the unconscious person to do some talking. It is simply necessary to reverse any flow to make unconsciousness disappear. But this is normally cared for in modern Scientology by running the Trio above.

"The idea here is to give
the preclear nothing but wins and to refrain
from giving the preclear losses in
the game of processing. Thus it can be seen
that processing is a team activity..."

THE FUTURE OF SCIENTOLOGY

THE FUTURE OF SCIENTOLOGY

WITH MAN NOW EQUIPPED with weapons sufficient to destroy all Mankind on Earth, the emergence of a new religion capable of handling Man is vital. Scientology is such a religion. It was born in the same crucible as the atomic bomb. The basic intelligence of Scientology came from nuclear physics, higher mathematics and the understanding of the Ancients in the East. Scientology can do exactly what it says it can do.

With Scientology, Man can prevent insanity, criminality and war. It is for Man to use. It is for the betterment of Man.

Today, the primary race of Earth is not between one nation and another. The only race that matters at this moment is the one being run between Scientology and the atomic bomb. The history of Man, as has been said by well-known authorities, may well depend upon which one wins.

FINIS

$\mathcal{A}$PPENDIX

𝓕URTHER STUDY
BOOKS & LECTURES BY L. RON HUBBARD

The materials of Dianetics and Scientology comprise the largest body of information ever assembled on the mind, spirit and life, rigorously refined and codified by L. Ron Hubbard through five decades of research, investigation and development. The results of that work are contained in hundreds of books and more than 3,000 recorded lectures. A full listing and description of them all can be obtained from any Scientology Church or Publications Organization. (See *Guide to the Materials*.)

The books and lectures below form the foundation upon which the Bridge to Freedom is built. They are listed in the sequence Ron wrote or delivered them. In many instances, Ron gave a series of lectures immediately following the release of a new book to provide further explanation and insight of these milestones. Through monumental restoration efforts, those lectures are now available and are listed herein with their companion book.

While Ron's books contain the summaries of breakthroughs and conclusions as they appeared in the developmental research track, his lectures provide the running day-to-day record of research and explain the thoughts, conclusions, tests and demonstrations that lay along that route. In that regard, they are the complete record of the entire research track, providing not only the most important breakthroughs in Man's history, but the *why* and *how* Ron arrived at them.

Not the least advantage of a chronological study of these books and lectures is the inclusion of words and terms which, when originally used, were defined by LRH with considerable exactitude. Far beyond a mere "definition," entire lectures are devoted to a full description of each new Dianetic or Scientology term—what made the breakthrough possible, its application in auditing as well as its application to life itself. As a result, one obtains a full conceptual understanding of Dianetics and Scientology and grasps the subjects at a level not otherwise possible.

Through a sequential study, you can see how the subject progressed and recognize the highest levels of development. The listing of books and lectures below shows where *Scientology: The Fundamentals of Thought* fits within the developmental line. From there you can determine your *next* step or any earlier books and lectures you may have missed. You will then be able to fill in missing gaps, not only gaining knowledge of each breakthrough, but greater understanding of what you've already studied.

This is the path to knowing how to know, unlocking the gates to your future eternity. Follow it.

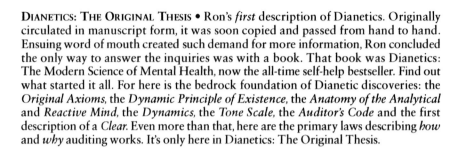

DIANETICS: THE ORIGINAL THESIS • Ron's *first* description of Dianetics. Originally circulated in manuscript form, it was soon copied and passed from hand to hand. Ensuing word of mouth created such demand for more information, Ron concluded the only way to answer the inquiries was with a book. That book was Dianetics: The Modern Science of Mental Health, now the all-time self-help bestseller. Find out what started it all. For here is the bedrock foundation of Dianetic discoveries: the *Original Axioms*, the *Dynamic Principle of Existence*, the *Anatomy of the Analytical* and *Reactive Mind*, the *Dynamics*, the *Tone Scale*, the *Auditor's Code* and the first description of a *Clear*. Even more than that, here are the primary laws describing *how* and *why* auditing works. It's only here in Dianetics: The Original Thesis.

DIANETICS: THE EVOLUTION OF A SCIENCE • This is the story of *how* Ron discovered the reactive mind and developed the procedures to get rid of it. Originally written for a national magazine—published to coincide with the release of Dianetics: The Modern Science of Mental Health—it started a wildfire movement virtually overnight upon that book's publication. Here then are both the fundamentals of Dianetics as well as the only account of Ron's two-decade journey of discovery and how he applied a scientific methodology to unravel the mysteries and problems of the human mind. And, hence, the culmination of Man's 10,000-year search.

DIANETICS: THE MODERN SCIENCE OF MENTAL HEALTH • The bolt from the blue that began a worldwide movement. For here is Ron's landmark book presenting his discovery of the *reactive mind* that underlies and enslaves Man. It's the source of nightmares, unreasonable fears, upsets and insecurity. And here is the way to get rid of it and achieve the long sought goal of Clear. This is the complete handbook of Dianetics procedure and, with it, any two reasonably intelligent people can break the chains that have held them prisoner to the upsets and trauma of the past. A bestseller for more than half a century and with tens of millions of copies in print, translated in more than fifty languages and used in more than 100 countries of Earth, *Dianetics* is indisputably the most widely read and influential book about the human mind ever written. And for that reason, it will forever be known as *Book One*.

DIANETICS LECTURES AND DEMONSTRATIONS • Immediately following the publication of *Dianetics,* LRH began lecturing to packed auditoriums across America. Although addressing thousands at a time, demand continued to grow. To meet that demand, his presentation in Oakland, California, was recorded. In these four lectures, Ron related the events that sparked his investigation and his personal journey to his groundbreaking discoveries. He followed it all with a personal demonstration of Dianetics auditing—the only such demonstration of Book One available, and invaluable to the Dianeticist. *4 lectures.*

DIANETICS PROFESSIONAL COURSE LECTURES—*A SPECIAL COURSE FOR BOOK ONE AUDITORS* • Following six months of coast-to-coast travel, lecturing to the first Dianeticists, Ron assembled auditors in Los Angeles for a new Professional Course. The subject was his next sweeping discovery on life—the *ARC Triangle,* describing the interrelationship of *Affinity, Reality* and *Communication.* Through a series of fifteen lectures, LRH announced many firsts, including the *Spectrum of Logic,* containing an infinity of gradients from right to wrong; *ARC and the Dynamics;* the *Tone Scales of ARC;* the *Auditor's Code* and how it relates to ARC; and the *Accessibility Chart* that classifies a case and how to process it. Here, then, is both the final statement on Book One Auditing Procedures and the discovery upon which all further research would advance. The data in these lectures was thought to be lost for over fifty years and only available in student notes published in Notes on the Lectures. The original recordings have now been discovered making them broadly available for the first time. Life in its highest state, *Understanding,* is composed of Affinity, Reality and Communication. And, as LRH said, the best description of the ARC Triangle to be found anywhere is in these lectures. *15 lectures.*

SCIENCE OF SURVIVAL—*PREDICTION OF HUMAN BEHAVIOR* • In the concluding chapter of Dianetics, Ron detailed his next target of investigation—Plan B and research into *life force.* Based on the milestone *Theta-MEST Theory,* describing how theta (life) interacts with the physical universe (Matter, Energy, Space and Time), and built around the *Hubbard Chart of Human Evaluation,* Science of Survival provides the first accurate prediction of human behavior. Included on the chart are all the manifestations of an individual's survival potential graduated from highest to lowest, making this the complete book on the Tone Scale. Knowing only one or two characteristics of a person and using this chart, you can plot his or her position on the Tone Scale and thereby know the rest, obtaining an accurate index of their *entire* personality, conduct and character. Before this book the world was convinced that cases could not improve but only deteriorate. Science of Survival presents the idea of different states of case and exactly how one can progress upward on the Tone Scale. Combine it all and Science of Survival is the most useful book you will ever own.

THE SCIENCE OF SURVIVAL LECTURES • Underlying the development of the Tone Scale and Chart of Human Evaluation was a monumental breakthrough: The *Theta-MEST Theory,* containing the explanation of the interaction between Life—*theta*—with the physical universe of Matter, Energy, Space and Time—*MEST.* In these lectures, delivered to students immediately following publication of the book, Ron gave the most expansive description of all that lies behind the Chart of Human Evaluation and its application in life itself. Moreover, here also is the explanation of how the ratio of *theta* and *en(turbulated)-theta* determines one's position on the Tone Scale and the means to ascend to higher states. *4 lectures.*

SELF ANALYSIS—*THE BASIC SELF-PROCESSING HANDBOOK* • The barriers of life are really just shadows. Learn to know yourself—not just a shadow of yourself. Containing the most complete description of consciousness, Self Analysis takes you through your past, through your potentials, your life. First, with a series of self-examinations and using the Hubbard Chart of Human Evaluation, you plot yourself on the Tone Scale. Then, applying a series of light yet powerful processes, you embark on the great adventure of self-discovery. This book further contains embracive principles that reach *any* case, from the lowest to the highest—including auditing techniques so effective they are referred to by Ron again and again through all following years of research into the highest states. In sum, this book not only moves one up the Tone Scale but can pull a person out of almost anything.

ADVANCED PROCEDURE AND AXIOMS • With new breakthroughs on the nature and anatomy of engrams—"Engrams are effective only when the individual himself determines that they will be effective"—came the discovery of the being's use of a *Service Facsimile*: a mechanism employed to explain away failures in life, but which then locks a person into detrimental patterns of behavior and further failure. In consequence came a new type of processing addressing *Thought, Emotion* and *Effort* detailed in the "Fifteen Acts" of Advanced Procedure and oriented to the rehabilitation of the preclear's *Self-determinism*. Hence, this book also contains the all-encompassing, no-excuses-allowed explanation of *Full Responsibility*, the key to unlocking it all. Moreover, here is the codification of *Definitions, Logics*, and *Axioms*, providing both the summation of the entire subject and direction for all future research. *See Handbook for Preclears, written as a companion self-processing manual to Advanced Procedure and Axioms.*

THOUGHT, EMOTION AND EFFORT • Contained herein is all that stands behind the discovery and codification of the Logics and Axioms. And with that codification of the Axioms came the means to address key points on a case that could unravel all aberration. *Thought, Emotion, Effort, Basic Postulates, Prime Thought, Cause and Effect* and their effect on everything from *memory* and *responsibility* to an individual's own role in empowering *engrams*—these matters are only addressed in this series. Here, too, is the most complete description of the *Service Facsimile* found anywhere—and why its resolution removes an individual's self-imposed disabilities. *21 lectures.*

HANDBOOK FOR PRECLEARS—*THE ADVANCED SELF-PROCESSING HANDBOOK* • The "Fifteen Acts" of Advanced Procedure and Axioms are paralleled by the fifteen Self-processing Acts given in Handbook for Preclears. Moreover, this book contains several essays giving the most expansive description of the *Ideal State of Man*. Discover why behavior patterns become so solidly fixed; why habits seemingly can't be broken; how decisions long ago have more power over a person than his decisions today; and why a person keeps past negative experiences in the present. It's all clearly laid out on the Chart of Attitudes—a milestone breakthrough that complements the Chart of Human Evaluation—plotting the ideal state of being and one's *attitudes* and *reactions* to life. *In self-processing, Handbook for Preclears is used in conjunction with Self Analysis.*

THE LIFE CONTINUUM • Besieged with requests for lectures on his latest breakthroughs, Ron replied with everything they wanted and more at the Second Annual Conference of Dianetic Auditors. Describing the technology that lies behind the self-processing steps of the *Handbook*—here is the *how* and *why* of it all: the discovery of *Life Continuum*—the mechanism by which an individual is compelled to carry on the life of another deceased or departed individual, generating in his own body the infirmities and mannerisms of the departed. Combined with auditor instruction on use of the Chart of Attitudes in determining how to enter every case at the proper gradient, here, too, are directions for dissemination of the Handbook and hence, the means to begin wide-scale clearing. *10 lectures.*

SCIENTOLOGY: MILESTONE ONE • Ron began the first lecture in this series with six words that would change the world forever: "This is a course in *Scientology.*" From there, Ron not only described the vast scope of this, a then brand-new subject, he also detailed his discoveries on past lives. He proceeded from there to the description of the first E-Meter and its initial use in uncovering the *theta line* (the entire track of a thetan's existence), as entirely distinct from the *genetic body line* (the time track of bodies and their physical evolution), shattering the "one-life" lie and revealing the *whole track* of spiritual existence. Here, then, is the very genesis of Scientology. *22 lectures.*

THE ROUTE TO INFINITY: TECHNIQUE 80 LECTURES • As Ron explained, "Technique 80 is the *To Be or Not To Be* Technique." With that, he unveiled the crucial foundation on which ability and sanity rest: *the being's capacity to make a decision*. Here, then, is the anatomy of "maybe," the *Wavelengths of ARC*, the *Tone Scale of Decisions*, and the means to rehabilitate a being's ability *To Be*...almost *anything. 7 lectures. (Knowledge of Technique 80 is required for Technique 88 as described in Scientology: A History of Man—below.)*

SCIENTOLOGY: A HISTORY OF MAN • "A cold-blooded and factual account of your last 76 trillion years." So begins A History of Man, announcing the revolutionary *Technique 88* — revealing for the first time the truth about past life — "whole track" — experience and the exclusive address, in auditing, to the thetan. Here is history unraveled with the first E-Meter, delineating and describing the principal incidents on the whole track to be found in any human being: *Electronic implants, entities,* the *genetic track, between-lives incidents, how bodies evolved* and *why you got trapped in them* — they're all detailed here.

TECHNIQUE 88: INCIDENTS ON THE TRACK BEFORE EARTH • "Technique 88 is the most hyperbolical, effervescent, dramatic, unexaggeratable, high-flown, superlative, grandiose, colossal and magnificent technique which the mind of Man could conceivably embrace. It is as big as the whole track and all the incidents on it. It's what you apply it to; it's what's been going on. It contains the riddles and secrets, the mysteries of all time. You could bannerline this technique like they do a sideshow, but nothing you could say, no adjective you could use, would adequately describe even a small segment of it. It not only batters the imagination, it makes you ashamed to imagine anything," is Ron's introduction to you in this never-before-available lecture series, expanding on all else contained in History of Man. What awaits you is the whole track itself. *15 lectures.*

SCIENTOLOGY 8-80 • The *first* explanation of the electronics of human thought and the energy phenomena in any being. Discover how even physical universe laws of motion are mirrored in a being, not to mention the electronics of aberration. Here is the link between theta and MEST revealing what energy *is,* and *how* you *create* it. It was this breakthrough that revealed the subject of a thetan's *flows* and which, in turn, is applied in *every* auditing process today. In the book's title, "8-8" stands for *Infinity-Infinity,* and "0" represents the static, *theta.* Included are the *Wavelengths of Emotion, Aesthetics, Beauty and Ugliness, Inflow and Outflow* and the *Sub-zero Tone Scale* — applicable only to the thetan.

SOURCE OF LIFE ENERGY • Beginning with the announcement of his new book — Scientology 8-80 — Ron not only unveiled his breakthroughs of theta as the Source of Life Energy, but detailed the *Methods of Research* he used to make that and every other discovery of Dianetics and Scientology: the *Qs* and *Logics* — methods of *thinking* applicable to any universe or thinking process. Here, then, is both *how to think* and *how to evaluate all data and knowledge,* and thus, the linchpin to a full understanding of both Scientology and life itself. *14 lectures.*

THE COMMAND OF THETA • While in preparation of his newest book and the Doctorate Course he was about to deliver, Ron called together auditors for a new Professional Course. As he said, "For the first time with this class we are stepping, really, beyond the scope of the word *Survival*." From that vantage point, the Command of Theta gives the technology that bridges the knowledge from 8-80 to 8-8008, and provides the first full explanation of the subject of *Cause* and a permanent shift of orientation in life from MEST to *Theta*. *10 lectures.*

SCIENTOLOGY 8-8008 • The complete description of the behavior and potentials of a *thetan*, and textbook for the *Philadelphia Doctorate Course* and *The Factors: Admiration and the Renaissance of Beingness* lectures. As Ron said, the book's title serves to fix in the mind of the individual a route by which he can rehabilitate himself, his abilities, his ethics and his goals—the attainment of *infinity* (8) by the reduction of the apparent *infinity* (8) of the MEST universe to *zero* (0) and the increase of the apparent *zero* (0) of one's own universe to *infinity* (8). Condensed herein are more than 80,000 hours of investigation, with a summarization and amplification of every breakthrough to date—and the full significance of those discoveries form the new vantage point of *Operating Thetan*.

THE PHILADELPHIA DOCTORATE COURSE LECTURES • This renowned series stands as the largest single body of work on the anatomy, behavior and potentials of the spirit of Man ever assembled. In complete detail, here is the thetan's relationship to the *creation, maintenance* and *destruction of universes*. In just those terms, here is the *anatomy* of matter, energy, space and time, and *postulating* universes into existence. Here, too, is the thetan's fall from whole track abilities and the *universal laws* by which they are restored. In short, here is Ron's codification of the upper echelon of theta beingness and behavior. Lecture after lecture fully expands every concept of the course text, Scientology 8-8008, providing the total scope of *you* in your true *native* state. *76 lectures and accompanying reproductions of the original 54 LRH hand-drawn lecture charts.*

THE FACTORS: ADMIRATION AND THE RENAISSANCE OF BEINGNESS • With the *potentials* of a thetan fully established came a look outward resulting in Ron's monumental discovery of a *universal solvent* and the basic laws of the theta *universe*—laws quite literally senior to anything: *The Factors: Summation of the Considerations of the Human Spirit and Material Universe*. So dramatic were these breakthroughs, Ron expanded the book Scientology 8-8008, both clarifying previous discoveries and adding chapter after chapter which, studied with these lectures, provide a postgraduate level to the Doctorate Course. Here then are lectures containing the knowledge of *universal truth* unlocking the riddle of creation itself. *18 lectures.*

THE CREATION OF HUMAN ABILITY—*A HANDBOOK FOR SCIENTOLOGISTS* • On the heels of his discoveries regarding the full potentialities of a thetan, came a year of intensive research and exploration into the realm of a *thetan exterior.* Through auditing and instruction, including 450 lectures in this same twelve-month span, Ron codified the entire subject of Scientology. And it's all contained in this handbook, from a *Summary of Scientology* to its basic *Axioms* and *Codes.* Moreover, here is *Intensive Procedure,* containing the famed Exteriorization Processes of *Route 1* and *Route 2* — processes drawn right from the Axioms. Each one is described in detail — *how* the process is used, *why* it works, the axiomatic technology that underlies its use, and the complete explanation of how a being can break the *false agreements* and *self-created barriers* that enslave him to the physical universe. In short, this book contains the ultimate summary of thetan exterior ability and its permanent accomplishment.

PHOENIX LECTURES: FREEING THE HUMAN SPIRIT • Here is the panoramic view of Scientology complete. Having codified the subject of Scientology in Creation of Human Ability, Ron then delivered a series of half-hour lectures to specifically accompany a full study of the book. From the *essentials* that underlie the technology — *The Axioms, Conditions of Existence* and *Considerations and Mechanics,* to the processes of *Intensive Procedure,* including twelve lectures describing one-by-one the thetan exterior processes of *Route 1* — it's all covered in full. Here then are the bedrock principles upon which everything in Scientology rests, including the embracive statement of the religion and its heritage — *Scientology, Its General Background. 42 lectures.*

DIANETICS 55!—*THE COMPLETE MANUAL OF HUMAN COMMUNICATION* • With all breakthroughs to date, a single factor had been isolated as crucial to success in every type of auditing. As LRH said, "Communication is so thoroughly important today in Dianetics and Scientology (as it always has been on the whole track) that it could be said if you were to get a preclear into communication, you would get him well." And this book delineates the *exact,* but previously unknown, anatomy and formulas for *perfect* communication. The magic of the communication cycle is *the* fundamental of auditing and the primary reason auditing works. The breakthroughs here opened new vistas of application — discoveries of such magnitude, LRH called Dianetics 55! the *Second Book* of Dianetics.

THE UNIFICATION CONGRESS: COMMUNICATION! FREEDOM & ABILITY • The historic Congress announcing the reunification of the subjects of Dianetics and Scientology with the release of *Dianetics 55!* Until now, each had operated in their own sphere: Dianetics addressed Man *as Man* — the first four dynamics, while Scientology addressed *life itself* — the Fifth to Eighth Dynamics. The formula which would serve as the foundation for all future development was contained in a single word: *Communication.* It was a paramount breakthrough Ron would later call, "the great discovery of Dianetics and Scientology." Here, then, are the lectures, as it happened. *16 lectures and accompanying reproductions of the original LRH hand-drawn lecture charts.*

SCIENTOLOGY: THE FUNDAMENTALS OF THOUGHT—*THE BASIC BOOK OF THE THEORY AND PRACTICE OF SCIENTOLOGY FOR BEGINNERS* • *(This current volume.)* Designated by Ron as the *Book One of Scientology.* After having fully unified and codified the subjects of Dianetics and Scientology came the refinement of their *fundamentals.* Originally published as a résumé of Scientology for use in translations into non-English tongues, this book is of inestimable value to both the beginner and advanced student of the mind, spirit and life. Equipped with this book alone, one can begin a practice and perform seeming miracle changes in the states of well-being, ability and intelligence of people. Contained within are the *Cycle-of-Action, Conditions of Existence, Eight Dynamics, ARC Triangle, Parts of Man,* the full analysis of *Life as a Game,* and more, including exact processes for individual application of these principles in processing. Here, then, in one book, are the very fundamentals of Scientology for application across one's entire life and the means to uplift the entire culture.

HUBBARD PROFESSIONAL COURSE LECTURES • While Fundamentals of Thought stands as an introduction to the subject for beginners, it also contains a distillation of fundamentals for every Scientologist. Here are the in-depth descriptions of those fundamentals, each lecture one-half hour in length and providing, one-by-one, a complete mastery of a single Scientology breakthrough—*Axioms 1-10; The Anatomy of Control; Handling of Problems; Start, Change and Stop; Confusion and Stable Data; Exteriorization; Valences* and more—the *why* behind them, *how* they came to be and their mechanics. And it's all brought together with the *Code of a Scientologist,* point by point, and its use in actually creating a new civilization. In short, here are the LRH lectures that make a *Professional Scientologist*—one who can apply the subject to every aspect of life. *21 lectures.*

ⲀDDITIONAL BOOKS
CONTAINING SCIENTOLOGY ESSENTIALS

WORK

THE PROBLEMS OF WORK—*SCIENTOLOGY APPLIED TO THE WORKADAY WORLD* • As Ron describes in this book, life is composed of seven-tenths work, one-tenth familial, one-tenth political and one-tenth relaxation. Here, then, is Scientology applied to that seven-tenths of existence including the answers to *Exhaustion* and the *Secret of Efficiency*. Here, too, is the analysis of life itself—a game composed of exact rules. Know them and you succeed. Problems of Work contains technology no one can live without, and that can immediately be applied by anyone in the workaday world.

LIFE PRINCIPLES

SCIENTOLOGY: A NEW SLANT ON LIFE • Scientology essentials for every aspect of life. Basic answers that put you in charge of your existence, truths to consult again and again: *Is It Possible to Be Happy?*, *Two Rules for Happy Living*, *Personal Integrity*, *The Anti-Social Personality* and many more. In every part of this book you will find Scientology truths that describe conditions in *your* life and *exact* ways to improve them.

AXIOMS, CODES AND SCALES

SCIENTOLOGY 0-8: THE BOOK OF BASICS • The companion to *all* Ron's books, lectures and materials. This is *the* Book of Basics, containing indispensable data you will refer to constantly: the *Axioms of Dianetics and Scientology; The Factors;* a full compilation of all *Scales*—more than 100 in all; listings of the *Perceptics* and *Awareness Levels;* all *Codes* and *Creeds* and much more. The senior laws of existence are condensed into this single volume, distilled from more than 15,000 pages of writings, 3,000 lectures and scores of books.

SCIENTOLOGY ETHICS:
TECHNOLOGY OF OPTIMUM SURVIVAL

INTRODUCTION TO SCIENTOLOGY ETHICS • A new hope for Man arises with the first workable technology of ethics – technology to help an individual pull himself out of the downward skid of life and to a higher plateau of survival. This is the comprehensive handbook providing the crucial fundamentals: *Basics of Ethics & Justice; Honesty; Conditions of Existence; Condition Formulas* from Confusion to Power; the *Basics of Suppression* and its handling; as well as *Justice Procedures* and their use in Scientology Churches. Here, then, is the technology to overcome any barriers in life and in one's personal journey up the Bridge to Total Freedom.

PURIFICATION

CLEAR BODY, CLEAR MIND – *THE EFFECTIVE PURIFICATION PROGRAM* • We live in a biochemical world, and this book is the solution. While investigating the harmful effects that earlier drug use had on preclears' cases, Ron made the major discovery that many street drugs, particularly LSD, remained in a person's body long after ingested. Residues of the drug, he noted, could have serious and lasting effects, including triggering further "trips." Additional research revealed that a wide range of substances – medical drugs, alcohol, pollutants, household chemicals and even food preservatives – could also lodge in the body's tissues. Through research on thousands of cases, he developed the *Purification Program* to eliminate their destructive effects. Clear Body, Clear Mind details every aspect of the all-natural regimen that can free one from the harmful effects of drugs and other toxins, opening the way for spiritual progress.

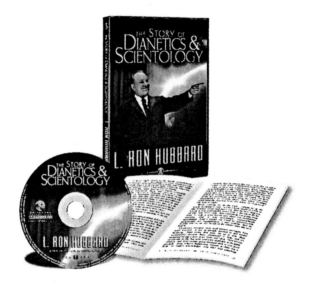

AND YOU CAN *MEET* L. RON HUBBARD

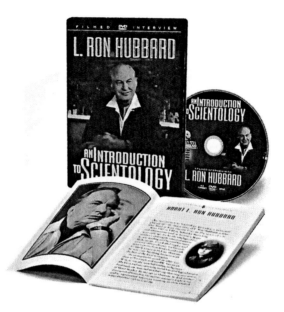

IN HIS *ONLY* FILMED INTERVIEW

What is Scientology?

What is the practical application of Scientology for the average man in the street?

How can Scientology help people overcome their problems?

Why is Man on this planet and what is his purpose here?

Such are the questions posed by millions and, in this rare filmed interview, Ron provided the answers: what *drove* his quest to help Mankind, his hard won *discoveries* providing the long sought answers to the riddles of the mind and life, and how he forged a *route* to accomplish new states of beingness and happiness—here it is as Ron himself explained it to the world.

Meet the man who founded a new religion in the atomic age, a religion that now spans the globe, a religion changing the face of Earth, a religion where science and religion finally meet and so ... a religion that could only have been called *Scientology.*

Get
An Introduction to Scientology

GET YOUR FREE
GUIDE TO THE
MATERIALS

- All books
- All lectures
- All reference books

All of it
laid out in
chronological
sequence with
descriptions of
what each
contains.

YOU'RE ON AN ADVENTURE! HERE'S THE MAP.

*Y*our journey to a full understanding of Dianetics and Scientology is the greatest adventure of all. But you need a map that shows you where you are and where you are going.

That map is the Materials Guide Chart. It shows all Ron's books and lectures with a full description of their content and subject matter so you can find exactly what *you* are looking for and precisely what *you* need.

New editions of all books include extensive glossaries, containing definitions for every technical term. And as a result of a monumental restoration program, the entire library of Ron's lectures are being made available on compact disc, with complete transcripts, glossaries, lecture graphs, diagrams and issues he refers to in the lectures. As a result, you get *all* the data and can learn with ease, not only gaining a full *conceptual* understanding, but each step of the way ascending to higher states of personal freedom.

To obtain your FREE Materials Guide Chart and Catalog, or to order L. Ron Hubbard's books and lectures, contact:

US AND INTERNATIONAL:
**Bridge
Publications, Inc.**
5600 E. Olympic Boulevard
Commerce, California 90022
www.bridgepub.com
Phone: 1-800-722-1733
Fax: 1-323-953-3328

UNITED KINGDOM AND EUROPE:
**New Era Publications
International ApS**
Smedeland 20
2600 Glostrup, Denmark
www.newerapublications.com
Phone: +800-808-8-8008
Fax: (45) 33 73 66 33

Books and lectures are also available direct from Churches of Scientology.
*See **Addresses**.*

187

$\mathcal{A}$DDRESSES

$\mathcal{S}$cientology is the fastest-growing religion in the world today. Churches and Missions exist in cities throughout the world, and new ones are continually forming.

To obtain more information or to locate the Church nearest you, visit the Scientology website:

www.scientology.org
e-mail: info@scientology.org

or

Phone: 1-800-334-LIFE
(for US and Canada)

You can also write to any one of the Continental Organizations, listed on the following page, who can direct you to one of the thousands of Churches and Missions world over.

L. Ron Hubbard's books and lectures may be obtained from any of these addresses or direct from the publishers on the previous page.

CONTINENTAL CHURCH ORGANIZATIONS:

UNITED STATES
CHURCH OF SCIENTOLOGY
CONTINENTAL LIAISON OFFICE
WESTERN UNITED STATES
1308 L. Ron Hubbard Way
Los Angeles, California 90027 USA
info@wus.scientology.org

CHURCH OF SCIENTOLOGY
CONTINENTAL LIAISON OFFICE
EASTERN UNITED STATES
349 W. 48th Street
New York, New York 10036 USA
info@eus.scientology.org

CANADA
CHURCH OF SCIENTOLOGY
CONTINENTAL LIAISON OFFICE
CANADA
696 Yonge Street, 2nd Floor
Toronto, Ontario
Canada M4Y 2A7
info@scientology.ca

LATIN AMERICA
CHURCH OF SCIENTOLOGY
CONTINENTAL LIAISON OFFICE
LATIN AMERICA
Federacion Mexicana de Dianetica
Calle Puebla #31
Colonia Roma, Mexico D.F.
C.P. 06700, Mexico
info@scientology.org.mx

UNITED KINGDOM
CHURCH OF SCIENTOLOGY
CONTINENTAL LIAISON OFFICE
UNITED KINGDOM
Saint Hill Manor
East Grinstead, West Sussex
England, RH19 4JY
info@scientology.org.uk

AFRICA
CHURCH OF SCIENTOLOGY
CONTINENTAL LIAISON OFFICE AFRICA
5 Cynthia Street
Kensington
Johannesburg 2094, South Africa
info@scientology.org.za

AUSTRALIA, NEW ZEALAND & OCEANIA
CHURCH OF SCIENTOLOGY
CONTINENTAL LIAISON OFFICE ANZO
20 Dorahy Street
Dundas, New South Wales 2117
Australia
info@scientology.org.au

Church of Scientology
Liaison Office of Taiwan
1st, No. 231, Cisian 2nd Road
Kaohsiung City
Taiwan, ROC
info@scientology.org.tw

EUROPE
CHURCH OF SCIENTOLOGY
CONTINENTAL LIAISON OFFICE EUROPE
Store Kongensgade 55
1264 Copenhagen K, Denmark
info@scientology.dk

Church of Scientology
Liaison Office of Commonwealth
of Independent States
Management Center of Dianetics
and Scientology Dissemination
Pervomajskaya Street, House 1A
Korpus Grazhdanskoy Oboroni
Losino-Petrovsky Town
141150 Moscow, Russia
info@scientology.ru

Church of Scientology
Liaison Office of Central Europe
Nánási út 1/C
1031 Budapest, Hungary
info@scientology.hu

Church of Scientology
Liaison Office of Iberia
C/Miguel Menendez Boneta, 18
28460 - Los Molinos
Madrid, Spain
info@spain.scientology.org

Church of Scientology
Liaison Office of Italy
Via Cadorna, 61
20090 Vimodrone
Milan, Italy
info@scientology.it

GET A FREE
SIX-MONTH MEMBERSHIP
IN THE INTERNATIONAL
ASSOCIATION OF SCIENTOLOGISTS

*T*he International Association of Scientologists is the membership organization of all Scientologists united in the most vital crusade on Earth.

A free Six-Month Introductory Membership is extended to anyone who has not held a membership with the Association before.

As a member, you are eligible for discounts on Scientology materials offered only to IAS Members. You also receive the Association magazine, *IMPACT,* issued six times a year, full of Scientology news from around the world.

The purpose of the IAS is:

"To unite, advance, support and protect Scientology and Scientologists in all parts of the world so as to achieve the Aims of Scientology as originated by L. Ron Hubbard."

Join the strongest force for positive change on the planet today, opening the lives of millions to the greater truth embodied in Scientology.

JOIN THE INTERNATIONAL ASSOCIATION OF SCIENTOLOGISTS.

To apply for membership,
write to the International
Association of Scientologists
c/o Saint Hill Manor, East Grinstead
West Sussex, England, RH19 4JY

www.iasmembership.org

*É*DITOR'S GLOSSARY
OF WORDS, TERMS AND PHRASES

Words often have several meanings. The definitions used here only give the meaning that the word has as it is used in this book. Dianetics and Scientology terms appear in bold type. Beside each definition you will find the page on which it first appears, so you can refer back to the text if you wish.

This glossary is not meant to take the place of standard language or Dianetics and Scientology dictionaries, which should be referred to for any words, terms or phrases that do not appear below.

– The Editors

aberrated: affected by *aberration*. Aberrated conduct would be wrong conduct or conduct not supported by reason. Aberration is a departure from rational thought or behavior; not sane. *See also* **aberration**. Page 69.

aberration: mental derangement, departure from rational thought or behavior; not sane. From the Latin *aberrare,* to wander from; Latin, *ab,* away, *errare,* to wander. It means basically to err, to make mistakes or more specifically to have fixed ideas which are not true. The entire cause of aberration is contained in the discovery of the previously unknown *reactive mind.* Its entire anatomy and the eradication of its harmful effects (that cause aberration) are contained in the book *Dianetics: The Modern Science of Mental Health.* Page 72.

acknowledge: say or do something that informs another that his statement or action has been noted, understood and received. Page 148.

actingness: the state or condition of acting, exerting energy or force; doing. Page 71.

aggrandize: make important; increase the power, status or wealth of. Page 133.

agitated: troubled in mind; disturbed; excited. Page 158.

agitation: a disturbance of the mind often shown by physical excitement or restlessness. Page 154.

allness: the state or quality of being complete or inclusive of all or a whole; totality or entirety. Page 90.

anatomical: belonging to or connected with the study or practice of anatomy (the science of bodily structure). Page 73.

anatomy: structure or arrangement of the parts of something. Page 58.

anchor points: points which are anchored in a space different to the physical universe space around a body. Page 73.

Ancients, the: the civilized peoples, nations or cultures of ancient times. Page 169.

anesthetized: made unconscious as by an *anesthetic,* a substance that brings about unconsciousness or insensitivity to pain. Page 70.

antagonists: things, people, etc., opposing or in conflict with something or someone else. Page 160.

antidote: something that prevents or counteracts harmful or unwanted effects. Page 128.

antipathetic: feeling or expressing anger, hostility, strong opposition or disgust, especially toward a particular person or thing. Page 57.

antisocial: hostile to or disruptive of the established social order; of behavior that is harmful to the welfare of people generally. Page 2.

apparency: appears to be, as distinct from what actually *is.* Page 22.

appreciable: sufficient to be readily perceived or estimated. Page 163.

approximate: come near to; approach closely. Page 48.

apt: inclined; given to; likely. Page 88.

Aquinas, Saint Thomas: (1225–1274) Italian philosopher and religious scholar who insisted that reason and faith are fully compatible and complementary and that religion is the highest science. He professed that the human being consists of a soul and a body and that the soul survives after death. Page 5.

arbitrary: based on judgment or useful selection rather than on the fixed nature of something. Page 38.

arduous: requiring great exertion, energy, etc. Page 69.

arrant: that is plainly such; downright; thorough; complete. Page 95.

ascendancy: the quality or state of being in an elevated position. Page 90.

As-ising: causing something to vanish or cease to exist by viewing it exactly as it is. Page 161.

aspect: nature; quality; character. Page 153.

aspiration: goal or objective. Page 6.

assertion: a confident and forceful statement of fact or belief. Page 53.

assumption(s): 1. something accepted as true. Page 86.
2. taking upon oneself. Page 92.

assured: sure or certain. Page 90.

astral body: in spiritualism, the belief in a sort of spirit body or a "double" of the physical body. Spiritualists believed this astral body could be separated from the physical body and when it did so was composed of a spirit *and* mind *and* body. This is in contrast to Scientology where the thetan (spirit, the person himself) can *fully* detach, by itself, from both mind and body. Page 66.

at hand: soon or near in time. Also, close or nearby. Page 2.

atomic bomb: an extremely destructive type of bomb, the power of which results from the immense quantity of energy suddenly released with the splitting of the nuclei (centers) of atoms into fragments. Page viii.

atomic fission: the splitting (fissioning) of the nucleus (center) of an atom into fragments, accompanied by a tremendous release of energy—the principle of the atomic bomb. Page viii.

at their choice: in accordance with someone's selection, decision or determinism in regards to something. Page 6.

Attila: (?-A.D. 453) barbarian conqueror and king of the Huns (a warlike Asiatic people). With his armies, known and feared for their cruelty, Attila carried out wholesale destruction and merciless treatment of those he overran. He violently conquered Eastern and Central Europe, establishing a large empire. Page 95.

auditing: the activity by which the auditor listens and commands. Also called *processing*. Page 114.

auditor: a Scientology practitioner; one who listens, a listener. Page 6.

authoritarian: unwilling to change strongly held opinions; favoring acceptance without question of the opinion of an "expert" as opposed to acceptance based on observable facts. Page 15.

Authorship: the origination or instigation of an action, condition, etc.; specifically the being or act which brought the universe into existence. Page 76.

automaticity: something uncontrolled; anything that goes on running outside the control of the individual. Page 67.

axiom(s): a self-evident truth, as in geometry. There are fifty-eight Scientology Axioms and some two hundred Axioms of Dianetics which preceded the Scientology Axioms. Page 85.

barbarism: an absence of culture; uncivilized ignorance marked by wild, violent cruelty. Page 1.

barriers: spaces, energy movements or obstacles. Page 54.

baser: lower in value, place, position, degree, scale or rank. Page 46.

bedposts: the vertical posts at the corner of a bed, sometimes tall enough to support a canopy (rooflike covering of material over a bed). Page 122.

behold: hold in view; look at or observe. Page 22.

being: the result of having assumed an identity. Page 31.

beingness: condition or state of being; existence. Page 23.

beneath: situated directly below something and supporting it. Hence, at the foundation on which something stands, underlying and supporting it. Page 87.

bent upon: determined; set; resolved. Page 78.

be so: be in the condition or state just mentioned. Page 22.

besting: getting the better of, defeating, beating. Page 56.

between-lives areas: places where a thetan goes during the time between the loss of a body and taking on a new one. Page 77.

biochemical: of or pertaining to the science dealing with the chemical substances, processes and reactions that occur in living organisms. Page 74.

biophysics: the study of biological phenomena and problems using the principles and techniques of physics, such as the effects of radiation on living matter or the explanation of the transmission of nerve impulses, muscle contractions, etc. Page 73.

bizarre: very unusual or strange; odd; unexpected. Page 72.

black screens: mental pictures of blackness which prevent one from seeing pictures. Page 68.

blunted: weakened or impaired in force; made less effective. Page 79.

body worship: an excessive love, devotion or admiration for bodies; likened to the reverent love and devotion accorded to a god, idol or sacred object. Page 73.

bound up: literally, tied in the same bundle, meaning inseparably connected or associated. Page 127.

brigandage: the action of a bandit robbing travelers in mountains, forests or along roads, usually as a member of a roving band. Page 57.

burst in: suddenly and noisily interrupt somebody or something. Page 147.

but: only; just. Page 3.

by and large: in general; on the whole. Page 123.

capped: brought to a high point; completed. Page vii.

cart away: carry or take away some possession as if by putting it into a *cart*, a vehicle usually pulled by a horse. Page 127.

case(s): 1. all the content of the reactive mind. Page 115.
2. a general term for a person being audited or helped, particularly one who is being audited. Page 150.

cause: make something happen or come to be. Page 2.

cessation: a temporary or complete stopping; discontinuance. Page 77.

chant: say something monotonously or repetitiously. Page 54.

chemistry: the branch of science that deals with the identification of the substances of which matter is composed, the investigation of their properties and the ways in which they interact, combine and change, and the use of these processes to form new substances. Page vii.

China: a reference to early twentieth-century China, characterized by severe overpopulation, a high death rate and where some believed that human life was of little value. Page 95.

choice, at their: in accordance with someone's selection, decision or determinism in regards to something. Page 6.

clamor: an intense (and sometimes noisy) expression of desire or dissatisfaction. Page 90.

clarified: brought order into. Page 32.

close: (of an observation, experiment, examination, etc.) done in a careful and thorough way. Page 91.

closely: with little or no space or time intervening; near together; being near in relationship. Page 91.

closes: brings down to a smaller amount or extent; reduces, lessens. Page 124.

colored: influenced or distorted to some degree; caused to appear different from what something really is or should be. Page ix.

colors: alters, influences or distorts to some degree; causes to appear different from what is really there. Page 124.

commodity: something tangible and real, likened to raw material or a primary agricultural product that can be bought and sold. Page 54.

common denominator: something common to or characteristic of a number of people, things, situations, etc.; shared characteristic. Page 45.

communication bridge: communication bridge is described in the chapter Auditing: Procedures and Processes, section Auditing: Things to Avoid. Page 163.

communication lag: the length of time between the placing of the question by the auditor and the *answering of that exact question* by the preclear. Page 115.

communism: the political theory or system in which all property and wealth is owned by all the members of a classless society and a single party with absolute power runs the economic and political systems of the state. Extensive restrictions are enforced on personal and religious liberties and freedom, and individual rights are overruled by the collective needs of the masses. Page 66.

companies: military units of eighty to two hundred soldiers commanded by a captain. Page 56.

comparable: capable of being compared; having features in common with something else to permit or suggest comparison. Page 157.

composition: the way in which the whole of something is made, especially the manner in which its different parts are combined or related. From a Latin word which means placed together. Page 47.

compulsively: in a manner of acting under an irresistible impulse to perform an act that is contrary to one's own will. Page 66.

concentric: having a common center, as circles one within another. Page 40.

condensed: more dense or compact; said of a compressed area or volume. Page 47.

conditions: circumstances, qualities. Page 31.

condoned: forgave, pardoned, overlooked or accepted an offense, usually a serious one, without protest or complaint. Page 74.

consider: think, believe, suppose. Page 22.

consideration: a thought, belief, supposition or postulate. Page 21.

consists: 1. is made up or composed of. Page 23.
2. is characterized by. Page 149.

consume: to destroy totally, as by fire. Used figuratively. Page 1.

context: the words or passages of text that come before or after a particular word that help to explain or determine its full meaning; the general sense of a word or a clarification of it. Page 45.

contract: an agreement between two or more people for the doing or not doing of something specified (sometimes signed and enforceable by law). Page 87.

control mechanisms: means or systems for restraining, regulating or dominating others. Page 151.

counter: acting in opposition; lying or tending in the opposite direction; having an opposite tendency, to the opposite effect. Page 23.

counterfeits: gives a false appearance of. Page 77.

counterposed: placed in opposition. Page 58.

counterposition: a thing that is opposite to something else, as for contrast or balance. Page 159.

course(s): a particular succession or series of actions that somebody takes to achieve something; way of action. Page 69.

covert: hidden; not openly practiced, engaged in, etc. Page 46.

cravenness: a condition of being extremely cowardly; showing great weakness of will. Page 2.

creatingness: a reference to a lower level condition of creating, such as when starting a new creation to counter against an old creation, resulting in confusion and chaos, as in *"one is apt to get into a chaos of thinkingness, or creatingness, or livingness."* Page 101.

crises: times of (emotional) difficulty or instability requiring or leading to a decisive change. Page 148.

crucible: figuratively, a place in which forces interact to cause or influence development or change. Literally, a *crucible* is a pot (that may vary in size from a small laboratory utensil for chemical analysis to very large industrial equipment) in which metals or other substances can be melted or heated up to very high temperatures. Page 169.

cult: great or excessive devotion to some idea or thing; especially, such devotion regarded as offbeat and odd or temporary. Page 66.

curse: a cause of unhappiness or harm; a great evil. Page 54.

curve: a graphic representation of the variations caused in something by changing conditions, often drawn as a curve. Page 78.

decries: cries out against; expresses vigorous disapproval. Page 121.

delineated: described or outlined. Page 114.

derangement: disturbance of the functions of the mind; mental disorder. Page 65.

deranges: disturbs the order or arrangement of; upsets the normal condition or functioning of. Page 74.

descend: to move from a higher to a lower place; come or go down. Page 48.

desensitize: become less forceful or capable of emotional impact. Page 89.

despair: complete loss of hope regarding some thing or action; feelings of defeat. Page 126.

destruction: (in terms of action) a creation of something against a creation of something else. Page 22.

detached: separated; apart from. Page 66.

detached eye: *detached* in this sense means unaffected by emotional involvement or any form of bias. *Eye* here means a point of view or way of thinking. Hence, a *detached eye* is a point of view that is impartial or free from involvement. Page 53.

deter: discourage or restrain from acting or proceeding. Page 116.

dialectical: of or pertaining to *dialectic,* originally the practice of attempting to arrive at the truth by the exchange of logical arguments or back and forth questions and answers. Later, the word was used to describe the theory that the evolution of ideas occurs because a concept gives rise to its opposite and, as a result of this conflict, a third view – supposedly at a higher level of truth than the first two views – is obtained. German revolutionist Karl Marx (1818-1883) altered this, viewing life as material only and containing contradictory sides or aspects ("struggle of opposites"), the conflicts of which are the driving forces of change and eventually transform or dissolve these things. Page 6.

dialectical materialism: a theory adopted as the official philosophy of communism, based on the works of German revolutionist Karl Marx (1818-1883). The theory maintains that the material world has reality independent of the mind or spirit and ideas can arise only from material conditions. Marx asserted that everything is material, including human culture. He stated all things naturally contain contradictory sides or aspects, whose tension or conflict causes a "struggle of opposites" and this is the driving force of change and eventually transforms or dissolves all things. Page 6.

dichotomy: a pair of opposites; plus and minus; positive and negative. Page 153.

dictate: determine or command what will be done. Page 69.

dilettante: related to taking up an art, activity or subject merely for amusement, especially in a superficial way. Said of one who interests himself in an art or science merely as a pastime and without serious aim or study. Page 2.

dimension: measurable or spatial extent of any kind, as length, width and height. Page 86.

discharged: released or dismissed from a job. Page 26.

discourses: verbal interchanges of ideas; conversations. Page 48.

disdains: despises, hates; considers unworthy of oneself. Page 91.

disparagement: the expression of a low opinion of something; the act of discrediting somebody or something. Page 116.

dispense: to do away with; do without; give up the possession of. Page 152.

disposition: arrangement or placing; a putting in order. Page 32.

dissertations: extended, usually systematic oral or written treatments of a subject. Page 80.

dissuaded: talked out of doing, thinking, believing or feeling something. Page 2.

divisible: capable of being separated into parts or sections; separable. Page 65.

doing: action, function, accomplishment, the attainment of goals, the fulfilling of purpose or any change of position in space. Page 32.

dopiness: mental slowness or confusion; drowsiness. Page 154.

drafted: chosen or taken for required military service by drawing from a group. Page 60.

drills: exercises, processes. Page 6.

drowns: overwhelms or causes to disappear as if by submerging in water. Page 124.

dug up: gotten out of the ground by digging. Used figuratively to mean found; obtained; searched out. Page 124.

duress: compulsion to do or not to do something resulting from pressure, force or threats. Page 70.

dwelling upon: spending time upon or lingering over (a thing) in action or thought; remaining with the attention fixed on. Page 58.

dwindling spiral: the worse someone (or something) gets, the more capacity they have to get worse. *Spiral* here refers to a progressive downward movement, marking a relentlessly deteriorating state of affairs and considered to take the form of a spiral. The term comes from aviation where it is used to describe the phenomenon of a plane descending and spiraling in smaller and smaller circles, as in an accident or feat of expert flying which, if not handled, can result in loss of control and a crash. Page 57.

East, the: used to refer to the southern and eastern part of Asia, including India, China and Japan. Page 169.

eccentricities: oddities or peculiarities; deviations from what is ordinary or customary, as in conduct or manner. Page 69.

effected: brought about; produced as a result; caused. Page 74.

electrical field: a region, volume or space where a specific, measurable electrical influence, force, etc., exists. Page 73.

emanation: an act or instance of flowing out, proceeding, as from a source or origin. Page 91.

E-Meter: short for *electropsychometer,* a specially designed instrument used by an auditor which helps locate long-hidden sources of travail. It does not diagnose or cure anything; it simply measures the mental state or change of state of an individual.

employed: made use of; applied. Page 6.

employs: applies (a thing) to some definite purpose; uses as a means to achieve something. Page 163.

engineering: the branch of science and technology concerned with the design, construction and use of engines, machines and structures. Page 15.

ensue(s): 1. follow as a consequence or result. Page 126.
2. follows in order; comes afterward, especially in immediate succession. Page 163.

entity: a thing that has independent or separate or self-contained existence; something that exists as a particular unit. Page 68.

equilateral: all sides the same. Page 47.

erasing: vanishing out of the reactive mind. Page 161.

err: make mistakes, be incorrect. Page 123.

established: shown to be valid or true; proved. Page 25.

estimation(s): 1. judgments or calculations as to the value, amount, time, size, etc., of something. Page 68.
2. opinion or judgment. Page 107.

euthanasia: the right to kill people who were considered to be a burden on a society. Page 74.

evaluate: to conclude for or tell a preclear what is wrong with him or what to think about his case. Page 115.

evolution: the idea that all living things evolved from simple organisms and changed through the ages to produce millions of different species: the theory that development of a species or organism from its original or primitive state to its present specialized state includes adaption (form or structure modified to fit a changed environment). Page 76.

evolutionaries: those who believe in the possibility of social progress by peaceful means. Page 1.

exact sciences: sciences (such as mathematics or physics), in which facts can be accurately observed and results can be accurately predicted. Page vii.

exciting: arousing or causing (comment, reaction, etc.). Page 153.

existence: apparency, reality, livingness. Page 31.

exploitation: unfair treatment or use of somebody or something, usually for personal gain. Page 2.

exterior: 1. situated outside. Page 53.
2. outdoors (as contrasted with indoors). Page 153.

exteriorization: exteriorization is explained in the chapter The Parts of Man, section The Spirit. Page 70.

exteriorize: the term *exteriorize* is explained in the chapter The Parts of Man, section The Spirit. Page 67.

exteriorizes: places or situates one outside of or external to something. Page 70.

face of it, on the: from appearances alone; apparently, seemingly. Page 91.

facet(s): any one of the several parts or sides of something; a particular aspect of a thing. Page 39.

factionalism: a condition characterized by the formation of *factions,* self-seeking groups of people inside a group, organization, political party, etc., working in a common cause against other such groups or against the main body. Page 3.

fallacy: a false or erroneous idea. Page 162.

fanaticism: an extreme and often irrational enthusiasm or belief on some subject. Page 95.

fancied: imagined; unreal or imaginary. Page 2.

fatal: descriptive of conditions, circumstances, or events that have caused or are bound to cause misfortune or failure. Page 159.

ferocious: characterized by extreme destructiveness; violently aggressive. Page 3.

field: a region or space where a specific, measurable influence, force, etc., exists. Page 73.

finis: the end; finish; conclusion. Used at the end of some books and films. *Finis* is Latin for end, utmost limit, highest point. Page 169.

fires: burning passions or feelings, especially of rage, hate, love or the like. Page 1.

fixated: having the attention commanded exclusively or repeatedly (on something); obsessively preoccupied. Page 125.

flat: no longer producing change or a reaction. When a present time problem is flat, the preclear does not feel he has to do anything about the problem such as go handle it. Page 157.

flow(s): a transfer of energy from one point to another. Page 73.

foremost: in the front or first position or place. Page 87.

forerunner: something that precedes the coming or development of someone or something else; literally, a person who goes in advance to announce the coming of someone or something that follows. Page 5.

found: became aware of; discovered. Page 149.

foundations: institutions financed by donations or legacies (money or property left by a will) to aid research, education, the arts, etc. Page vii.

frame of mind: a mental or emotional attitude or mood at a particular time; a state of mind. Page 126.

Frederick of Prussia: Frederick II (1712-1786), king of Prussia, a kingdom in northern Europe and the dominant state of what became the German empire. On the death of his father in 1740 Frederick became king and immediately began efforts to expand Prussia by invading other territories, soon making it the greatest military power in Europe. Page 95.

free-for-all: describing a disorganized fight, open to everyone and usually without rules. Page 133.

French Revolution: a revolt in France from 1789 to 1799 which overthrew the royal family and the aristocratic class and system of privileges they enjoyed. The revolution was in part a protest against France's absolute monarchy, entrenched and unproductive nobility and the consequent lack of freedom for the middle classes. During the revolution, 300,000 people were arrested and 17,000 were beheaded under the guillotine. Page 57.

fruition: attainment of anything desired; accomplishment. Page viii.

Genghis Khan: (1162?-1227) Mongol conqueror who founded the largest land empire in history and whose armies, known for their use of terror, conquered many territories and slaughtered the populations of entire cities. Page 95.

George Washington University: a private university, founded in 1821, in the city of Washington, DC, USA. Named after the first president of the United States, George Washington (1732-1799), it maintains various schools of education, including the School of Engineering and Applied Science. The university has a long history of supporting research in physics and other technical fields. Page vii.

germinate: begin to grow, develop; come into existence. Page 1.

get an idea of your (his) own: instead of copying, saying or doing something which another has already said or done, get an original idea, action or saying of your own. Page 95.

get into (things): to become occupied with, interested, involved or absorbed in (something). Page 60.

get out of (things): to avoid, escape or get away from. Page 60.

gives: yields or furnishes as a product, consequence or effect. Page 45.

glandular: of or relating to the glands (cells, groups of cells or organs in the body producing a secretion). For example, adrenal glands produce *adrenaline,* a hormone that is released into the bloodstream in response to physical or mental stress, as from fear of injury. It initiates many bodily responses, including stimulation of heart action and increase in blood pressure. Page 71.

grant: give, allow. Page 32.

grasp: to seize and hold by clasping with the fingers or arms. Hence, to take hold of intellectually; to seize and hold an idea firmly; comprehend. Page 147.

Gray's Anatomy: a standard text on the structure of the body compiled by British anatomist Henry Gray and first published in 1858. Page 73.

guise: outward appearance or form of someone or something. Page 56.

hand, at: soon or near in time. Also, close or nearby. Page 2.

harangue: to engage in any long, intense speech (or writing) that teaches a lesson or instructs in a bullying manner. Page 3.

hasten: cause something to happen quickly or sooner than it otherwise would. Page 74.

havingness: owning, possessing, being capable of commanding, positioning, taking charge of objects, energies or spaces. The essential definition of having is to be able to touch or permeate or to direct the disposition of. Page 32.

H-bombs: *hydrogen bombs,* explosive weapons of mass destruction (far more destructive than atomic bombs) in which huge amounts of energy are released. Page 2.

heart: the vital or essential part; core. Page 2.

heavenly bodies: objects that are in the sky such as stars or planets. Page 86.

hectically: frantically; in an agitated manner. Page 162.

held: judged to be; considered, regarded or thought to be. Page 80.

held down: kept down; kept under, restrained or checked. Page 7.

Hereafter: a future life, the world to come; a life or existence after death. Page 66.

hitherto: up to this time; until now. Page 68.

Hitler: Adolf Hitler (1889-1945), German political leader of the twentieth century who dreamed of creating a master race that would rule for a thousand years as the third German empire. Taking over rule of Germany by force in 1933 as a dictator, he began World War II (1939-1945), subjecting much of Europe to his domination and murdering millions of Jews and others considered "inferior." He committed suicide in 1945 when Germany's defeat was imminent. Page 95.

humanities: branches of learning concerned with human thought and relations, as distinguished from the sciences; especially literature, philosophy, history, etc. (Originally, *the humanities* referred to education that would enable a person to freely think and judge for himself, as opposed to a narrow study of technical skills.) Page vii.

-hungry: having, reflecting or characterized by an ardent desire or craving; longing eagerly (for), as in *attention-hungry*, craving or eagerly desiring attention. Page 123.

hypnotic trance: a state induced by hypnosis in which somebody is dazed or stunned or in some other way unaware of the environment and unable to respond. Page 70.

ideology: the doctrines, opinions or way of thinking of an individual, class, etc.; specifically, the body of ideas on which a particular political, economic or social system is based. Page 1.

immortal: not liable or subject to death; able to live or last forever. Page 77.

impart: communicate the knowledge of; make known or reveal. Page 116.

impinge: come in contact with; have an effect or impact on. Page 72.

implanted: fixed, established or embedded securely, as in the mind or consciousness. Page 70.

implements: tools and equipment used in doing any work; things employed in performing any activity. Page 95.

impression(s): the action involved in the pressure of one thing (often an external cause) upon or into the surface of another. Hence, a remembrance or mental picture of something impressed upon the mind as a consequence of experience. Page 68.

impressionable: capable of being impressed. *Impressed* means to have had a marked effect on the mind or emotions. Page 70.

incidence: the rate of occurrence of something, especially of something unwanted. Page 59.

inculcate: to fix deeply into someone's mind by repeated statement; instruct persistently. Page 94.

index: an indicator, sign or measure of something. Page 40.

indispensable: absolutely necessary or essential. Page 74.

individuality: the sum of the characteristics or qualities that sets one person apart from others; individual character. Page 38.

inexplicable: that cannot be explained, understood or accounted for. Page 70.

infinity: unlimited extent of time, space or quantity; unlimited capacity, energy, excellence or knowledge. Page 39.

initiated: started; caused (a process or action) to begin; brought into practice, use or creation. Page 79.

in practice: in the realm of action; practically, actually. Page 91.

inquiring: seeking facts, information or knowledge; wanting to know more. Page viii.

insofar: to the degree that; to such an extent that. Page 21.

intelligence quotient (IQ): a number arrived at by tests and intended to indicate a person's intelligence. (*Quotient* means the result of division, and refers to the way the test score is calculated.) Page 114.

interiorized: being inside something; stuck inside something. Page 88.

interjection: the act of putting something in between. Page 117.

intersperse: place at intervals among other things or in the course of something. Page 154.

in that: for the reason that. Page 58.

invade: to enter or penetrate. The statement, *"Scientology does not invade the Eighth Dynamic,"* is in reference to the fact that only when the individual has reached the Seventh (Spiritual) Dynamic in its entirety will he discover the true Eighth (God) Dynamic. Page 76.

invalidate: 1. to refute or degrade or discredit or deny something someone else considers to be a fact. Page 26.

2. to cause *invalidation,* a statement, action or inference that makes the preclear appear wrong. Page 115.

inverted: reversed in position, order or relationship from what is considered usual or normal. Page 66.

involuntary: a reference to involuntary muscular reactions, those that are normally not carried out by the individual's conscious choice such as the muscles of the digestive system. Page 71.

Jones, John: a common male name in America. Page 78.

junior: subordinate to; smaller in scale to something larger or more powerful. The use is military in origin and refers to an individual of lower position or rank. Page 56.

Kaiser Wilhelm: Kaiser Wilhelm II (1859-1941), the last emperor (Kaiser) of Germany who pursued an aggressive program of commercial and colonial expansion and who led Germany into World War I (1914-1918). Page 95.

keynote: the central or most important point or theme of something. Page 68.

keystone: a supporting principle; the chief element in a system; that upon which the remainder rests or depends. A *keystone* is the stone of an arch (typically the uppermost stone), which being the last put in, is regarded as keying or locking the whole structure together. Page 45.

Kingdom of Heaven: reference to the statement that appears in the Bible: "Repent: for the Kingdom of Heaven is at hand," meaning that Heaven is within reach or close by. *Kingdom* refers to the fact that God is the ruler over Heaven. Page 2.

knack: an acquired or natural skill of doing something successfully. Page 148.

knowingness: the state or quality of knowing. Page 68.

laid into: set, placed or deposited (into); placed in position (inside something). Page 69.

large, at: as a whole; in general. Page 66.

Last War of All: a reference to the potential total devastation of life on Earth such as would result from the use of atomic and hydrogen bombs. Page 1.

latterly: of late, recently. Page 66.

Leipzig University: a German university founded in 1409 in the city of Leipzig in east-central Germany, where Wilhelm Wundt, German psychologist, developed modern psychology. Page 5.

lethargy: lack of energy, activity or enthusiasm. Page 59.

literal: understanding things or acting in a strict, exact way without judgment. Page 69.

livingness: a reference to the act of existing without certainty, ability or knowing, where the individual considers that other influences can act upon him and that he can act upon other influences, as in *"one is apt to get into a chaos of thinkingness, or creatingness, or livingness."* Page 101.

loosely: not strictly; broadly. Page 56.

lowest (low) order: in a scale, the lowest, most inferior level or degree of quality or value that something has. Page 26.

magnitude: relative size, amount, importance, extent or influence. Page 157.

Man: the human race or species, humankind, Mankind. Page viii.

man: a human being, without regard to sex or age; a person. Page 58.

mania: wild or violent mental disorder; specifically, a condition characterized generally by abnormal excitability, exaggerated feelings of well-being, excessive activity or talkativeness, etc. Page 95.

maniac(s): a wildly or violently insane person; madman; lunatic. Page 126.

manifest: apparent to the senses, especially that of sight, or to the mind; evident; obvious. Page 67.

manifestation: a visible demonstration or display of the existence, presence, qualities or nature of something. Page 40.

Marxist: a supporter of the doctrines of German revolutionist Karl Marx (1818–1883) whose works were the basis of twentieth-century communism. He maintained that everything, thought, ideas and human culture, are material. Page 5.

mass(es): compounded, compressed energy particles; matter. Page 55.

maxim: a concisely expressed principle or rule of conduct, or a statement of a general truth. Page 59.

methodology: the methods or organizing principles underlying a particular art, science or other area of study. Page 114.

midnight: the final or darkest hour. Page 2.

misorientation: wrong or improper relationship to known facts or principles; wrong direction or tendency. Page 2.

monitored: controlled or regulated. Page 68.

morose: gloomy; depressed; sour-tempered. Page 78.

muck: anything unclean, worthless or degrading; literally, thick slimy mud. Page 1.

mutation: a sudden change in the hereditary (having to do with traits or characteristics transmitted from generation to generation through reproduction) material from a parent-type cell resulting in a new trait or characteristic in an organism, as distinguished from a variation resulting from generations of gradual change. Page 76.

Napoleon: Napoleon Bonaparte (1769–1821), French military leader. He rose to power in France by military force, declared himself emperor and conducted campaigns of conquest across Europe until his final defeat by armies allied against him in 1815. Half a million men died in the Napoleonic Wars of 1799–1815. Page 95.

neurons: cells that transmit nerve impulses and which are the basic functional units of the nervous system; also called *nerve cells*. Page 71.

nobles: people who are born into a high class who have special social or political status in a country. Page 57.

no-game conditions: no-game (and game conditions) are fully described in the chapter Game and No-Game Conditions. Page 54.

nothingness: Man is unable to define a "nothingness" without defining it in terms of a somethingness. So it's just a relative value. Nothing itself is no-thing. *Nothing* is defined as an absence of something. The suffix *-ness* is used when forming nouns expressing a state, quality or condition. Page 23.

not-know: to not remember or to forget; to decide that one does not know. Someone who is trying to overcome the painfulness of all that happened to him is trying to forget all about it and everything connected with it and push it out of his mind. This is an example of not-knowing. Page 101.

not-knowingness: being in present time and not in the past or the future. Page 155.

nuclear physics: that branch of physics that deals with the behavior, structure and component parts of the center of an atom (called a nucleus), which makes up almost all of the mass of the atom. Page vii.

numberless: too numerous to be counted. Page 26.

obsessively: in a manner pertaining to or resembling an obsession (the domination of one's thoughts or feelings by a persistent idea, image, desire, etc.). Page 148.

obstetrics: the branch of medicine concerned with childbirth and caring for and treating women in or in connection with childbirth. Page 74.

occasion: bring about; cause. Page 73.

old saw: an old saying, often repeated. Page 59.

operable: that operates; that is in effect; functions in a specified manner. Page 69.

optimum: most favorable or desirable, best. Page 67.

order: 1. methodical or harmonious arrangement; the condition in which a thing is in its proper place with reference to other things and to its purpose. Page 7.
2. sequence in respect to value, importance or some other criterion. Page 32.
3. a category, type, class or kind of thing of distinctive character or rank. Page 69.

order, lowest (low): in a scale, the lowest, most inferior level or degree of quality or value that something has. Page 26.

orthopedics: the branch of medicine concerned with the treatment of deformities, diseases and injuries of the bones, joints, muscles, etc. Page 74.

out-created: created against too thoroughly. Page 80.

outdistanced: literally, left behind, as in some kind of competition such as running. Hence, surpassed by a wide margin, especially through superior skill, knowledge or method. Page vii.

SCIENTOLOGY: THE FUNDAMENTALS OF THOUGHT • L. RON HUBBARD

outline: a general description covering the main points of something, such as a subject. Page 56.

out of repair: in need of fixing or correction, as in something damaged, worn or faulty; in bad condition. Page 161.

"out of the bottom": in Scientology, it describes an individual who drops down the Tone Scale so far he can go no further down. It symbolizes being worse off than merely being on the bottom of the ladder. Gone downward from the bottom. Page 162.

overwhelmed: overcome or overpowered in mind or feeling. Page 7.

palpable: easily perceptible by the mind or one of the senses, as to be almost able to be felt physically. *Palpable* comes from the Latin meaning "that can be touched." Page 54.

Pan-determinism: *pan* means *across* and *determinism* means the ability to determine the course of or the decision about. Hence, *Pan-determinism* means the willingness of an individual to determine the action of self and others. It means wider determinism than self. An individual who is Pan-determined is determined across the eight dynamics. Page 56.

panorama: a complete and comprehensive view or range. Page 53.

para-: runs alongside of; parallel, like or similar. Page 76.

paramount: the highest in rank or importance; chief. Page 73.

partisan: partial or biased to a specific thing, person, etc. Page 78.

party to, being a: being involved in as a member or participant. Page 24.

pastime: a specific form of amusement (as a recreation, game or sport). From the French term *passe-temps* meaning pass time. Page 53.

patently: clearly; plainly; obviously. Page 90.

peculiar: strange; unlike others, uncommon, unusual. Page 6.

permeate: to pass or spread into or through every part of something. Page 32.

persist: continue to exist; endure; remain. Page 86.

phenomena: things that appear or are perceived or observed; individual facts, occurrences or changes as perceived by any of the senses or by the mind: applied chiefly to a fact or occurrence, the cause or explanation of which is under observation or being scientifically described. Page 68.

physics: the science that deals with matter, energy, motion and force, including what these things are, why they behave as they do and the relationship between them, as contrasted to life sciences such as biology, which studies and observes living organisms such as animals and plants. Page vii.

playing fields (of life): the expanses or spaces where the actions of life are carried (played) out, likened to a *playing field*, a specified area of ground where individuals or teams compete (play) against each other. Page 88.

plot: to lay out or show some process, condition or course of something, as if with the precision used to chart the course of a ship, draw a map of an area, etc. Page 56.

plotting: arranging something beforehand (sometimes in a secret way). Page 60.

political: of or having to do with *politics,* the science or practice of government; the regulation and government of a nation or state for the preservation of its safety, peace and prosperity. *Government* is that controlling body of a nation, state or people which conducts its policy, actions and affairs. Page 1.

polo: a game played on horseback by two teams of four players each, who attempt to drive a small wooden ball through the opponents' goal. Page 53.

populace: the common people of a nation as distinguished from the higher classes. Page 57.

postulate: 1. to consider, to say a thing, and have it be true. Page 23. **2.** causative thinkingness. It is considering or saying something and having it be true. Page 60.

postulate, make a: to consider, to say a thing, and have it be true. Page 60.

practitioner: a person engaged in the practice of a profession. Page 6.

preclear: a person who is receiving auditing. Page 89.

preposterous: so contrary to nature, reason or common sense as to be laughable; absurd; ridiculous. Page 90.

presided over: having authority or control placed on or over. Page 68.

pressing: urging or insisting on; presenting earnestly. Page 2.

prevail: be in force, use or practice. Page 147.

prevailing: most frequent in amount; common. Page 92.

primitive: relating to a group or its members whose culture, through isolation, has remained at a basic uncomplicated level of social and economic organization. Page 94.

privates: soldiers of the lowest rank. Page 56.

problem: two or more purposes in opposition. Or intention-versus-intention. Page 1.

procedure: an established, precise and correct method of how one goes about something; an exact series of steps taken to accomplish an end. Page 147.

process: audit, drill. Page 7.

processes: exercises that bring about changes for the better in intelligence, behavior and general competence. Processes are best given in a small number of consecutive days, such as twenty-five hours in one week. Page 6.

processing: the verbal exercising of a preclear in exact Scientology processes. Also called *auditing*. Page 7.

progressive: characterized by progress, devoted to continuous improvement such as making use of new ideas, inventions, opportunities, experimentation and innovation. Page 123.

prone to: likely to or liable to suffer from, do or experience something, typically something regrettable or unwelcome. Page 79.

province: sphere or field of activity or authority. Page 73.

pseudo-psychology: false (pseudo) psychology, a reference to modern psychology, founded by German physiologist Wilhelm Wundt (1832-1920), an alteration of the subject which was originally a study of the psyche or soul. Page 6.

psychoanalysis: a system of mental therapy developed by Sigmund Freud (1856-1939) in Austria in 1894 in which the patient was made to talk about and recall, for years, incidents from his childhood believed by Freud to be the cause of mental ills. Page 113.

psychosomatic: *psycho* refers to mind and *somatic* refers to body; the term *psychosomatic* means the mind making the body ill or illnesses which have been created physically within the body by the mind. A description of the cause and source of psychosomatic ills is contained in *Dianetics: The Modern Science of Mental Health.* Page 7.

purveyors: ones who provide, supply or furnish something. Page 123.

puts up with: bears, endures or tolerates (anything disagreeable, painful, etc.). Page 93.

race: 1. humanity considered as a whole, as in the human race. Page 2.
2. a group of persons related by common history, nationality, geographic distribution or physical characteristics (color, facial features, size, etc.). Page 38.

radioactive: used to describe a substance that sends out harmful energy in the form of streams of very small particles due to the decay (breaking down) of atoms within the substance. This energy can be damaging or fatal to the health of people exposed to it. Page 2.

ramifications: effects, consequences or results. Page 152.

randomities: plural of *randomity,* unpredicted motion. It is a ratio: the amount of predicted motion in ratio to the amount of unpredicted motion which the individual has. He likes to have about 50 percent predicted motion and about 50 percent unpredicted motion. Page 96.

reason: sound judgment; good sense. Page 1.

recount: tell someone about something; give a description of an event or experience. Page 161.

recourse: turning to something for assistance. Page 72.

registered: recorded or made an impression, such as in the mind. Page 70.

render: 1. furnish; provide. Page 116.
2. cause to be or become; make. Page 164.

repair, out of: in need of fixing or correction, as in something damaged, worn or faulty; in bad condition. Page 161.

requisite: that which is required or necessary. Page 147.

restimulation: the action of something being reactivated; stimulated again. *Re-* means again and *stimulate* means to bring into action or activity. Page 70.

revolutionaries: people who advocate, work for or participate in a *revolution*, an overthrow or rejection and thorough replacement of an established government or political system, usually by the people governed. Page 1.

role: the part, character or function played or performed by a person in society or life. Page 2.

rudimentary: existing at an elementary or basic level. Page 89.

ruggedly: strongly; sturdily. Page 69.

rule, as a (general): normally; usually. Page 91.

run down: diminish or decrease (gradually or progressively). Page 156.

run out: erase; exhaust the negative influence of something. Page 125.

Saint Thomas Aquinas: (1225-1274) Italian philosopher and religious scholar who insisted that reason and faith are fully compatible and complementary and that religion is the highest science. He professed that the human being consists of a soul and a body and that the soul survives after death. Page 5.

sake of, for the: for the purpose or end of. Page 2.

savagery: an uncivilized state or condition marked by violent cruelty. Page 94.

saw: an old saying, often repeated. Page 59.

scan: to search a text quickly or systematically for particular information or features. Page 15.

scarcity: an insufficient amount or supply; shortage. Page 121.

scholars: those who have a great deal of knowledge in a particular branch of learning, especially in the field of literature or philosophy; those who have engaged in advanced study and acquired detailed knowledge in some special field and who engage in the analysis and interpretation of such knowledge. Page 95.

science: knowledge; comprehension or understanding of facts or principles, classified and made available in work, life or the search for truth. A science is a connected body of demonstrated truths or observed facts systematically organized and bound together under general laws. It includes trustworthy methods for the discovery of new truth within its domain and denotes the application of scientific methods in fields of study previously considered open only to theories based on subjective, historical or undemonstrable, abstract criteria. The word *science,* when applied to Scientology, is used in this sense—the most fundamental meaning and tradition of the word—and not in the sense of the *physical* or *material* sciences. Page 96.

scientific: accurate in the manner of an exact science. Page 54.

scientifically: systematically, methodically, thoroughly, accurately; in the manner of a science. Page 39.

score of things (on the): where things stand; in regard to the facts of the matter. Page 160.

searing: scorching or burning with intense heat. Page 2.

seeming: appearing to be; giving the impression of. Page viii.

self-recognition: acknowledgment or perception of the existence of self as an individual or spirit. Page 66.

senior: superior; of greater influence; on a higher level than (something). The use is military in origin and refers to an individual holding a position of higher rank. Page 56.

session: a period of time devoted to auditing. Page 115.

setting forth: presenting or declaring something; laying something out. Page 38.

shelved: laid aside as if on a shelf, put away as if done with. Page 102.

shortcomings: faults or failures to meet a certain standard, typically in a person's character or conduct. Page 40.

shuns: keeps away from (a place, person, object, etc.), avoids deliberately. Page 57.

significances: ideas, reasons, meanings, things considered, as opposed to the mass of the things. Page 162.

slavishly: in a manner showing no attempt at originality or independence of thought; blindly dependent on somebody else; excessively obedient, as a slave. Page 95.

solidities: things which are solid, firm or hard. Page 46.

solvent: something which solves or settles; something which has the power to cause to disappear or vanish such things as problems, situations or the like. Page 47.

somatic: *somatic* means, actually, *bodily* or *physical*. Because the word *pain* is restimulative, and because the word *pain* has in the past led to a confusion between physical pain and mental pain, the word *somatic* is used in Dianetics to denote physical pain or discomfort of any kind. It can mean actual pain, such as that caused by a cut or a blow; or it can mean discomfort, as from heat or cold; it can mean itching—in short, anything physically uncomfortable. It does not include mental discomfort such as grief. Hard breathing would not be a somatic. *Somatic* means a non-survival physical state of being. Page 68.

sorrow: mental and emotional suffering caused by loss or disappointment; sadness, grief or regret. Page 53.

sound: free from error; good, strong, valid. Page 116.

sovereignty: freedom from outside interference and the right to self-government. Page 3.

specialized: designed or existing for use in one particular line, area or subject. Page 87.

spiritualists: those who believe in *spiritualism,* the doctrine or belief that the spirits of the dead can and do communicate with the living, especially through another person known as a medium. Page 66.

statecraft: the art of government or the art of conducting state affairs. Page 2.

steerage: the part of a ship containing the machinery for steering; hence, guidance or direction. Page 93.

stern: hard, harsh or severe in manner or character. Page 126.

stimuli: plural of *stimulus.* Stimulus is any action or agent that causes or changes an activity in an organism, organ or part, as something that starts a nerve impulse, activates a muscle, etc. Page 68.

stimulus-response: a certain stimulus (something that rouses a person or thing to activity or energy or that produces a reaction in the body) automatically giving a certain response. Page 68.

subdued: those who have been defeated or overpowered by physical force or sometimes persuasion. Page 94.

subjective: inside the mind only. Page 160.

subject (to): that can be affected or influenced or controlled by a particular thing. Page 67.

subordinate: of less or secondary importance. Page 128.

succeedingly: coming next in order; subsequently. Page 47.

successively: in succession, following one upon another. Page 40.

summation: a summing up and statement of the value or qualities of. Page vii.

synthetic: not real or genuine; artificial. Page 59.

take to: develop a liking for; develop an ability for. Page 93.

taking sides: giving one's support to one person or group in contrast to that of an opposing one; being partial to one side. Page 57.

tenets: principles, doctrines, beliefs, etc., especially ones held true by members of a group, profession or movement. Page 77.

terminology: the system of terms belonging to any science or specialized subject. Page 113.

therapeutic: having a good effect on; contributing to a sense of well-being; beneficial. Page 7.

thinkingness: the act of worry-worry or figure-figure (endless worrying about something or trying to figure something out). Thinkingness is based upon the fact that a person doesn't know, so has to think about it. The solution depends upon the fact of one postulating that he does know, and then knows. In order to do thinking, one has to assume he has to go through some kind of a process in order to arrive at an answer. Hence, if a person doesn't know, he has to think about it. As in, *"one is apt to get into a chaos of thinkingness, or creatingness, or livingness."* Page 101.

thunderclap: literally a crash of thunder. Used figuratively to mean something resembling a thunderclap, as in loudness, unexpectedness or power. Page 2.

time continuum: a *continuum* is a continuous extent, series or whole, no part of which can be distinguished from neighboring parts except by arbitrary division. A *time continuum* is an agreed-upon uniform rate of change. Page 140.

time stream: of or pertaining to time thought of as a continuous flowing progression. Page 153.

time track: the length and breadth of existence in time. Page 77.

tone(s): one's emotional level. Page 46.

Tone Scale: a scale of emotional tones which shows the levels of human behavior. These tones, ranged from the highest to the lowest, are in part Serenity, Enthusiasm, Conservatism, Boredom, Antagonism, Anger, Covert Hostility, Fear, Grief and Apathy. Page 46.

too short a view: in a state or condition whereby something is examined, inspected or looked at from a particular position which is too close or doesn't extend far enough away from the observer. Hence, the phrase *processed up too short a view* means to process or audit someone where his attention is too close to where he is and not far enough outwards giving him a *longer* view. Page 162.

trance: also called *hypnotic trance,* a state induced by hypnosis in which somebody is dazed or stunned or in some other way unaware of the environment and unable to respond. Page 70.

transcended: gone beyond or risen above. Page 90.

travail: pain or suffering resulting from conditions which are mentally or physically difficult to overcome. Page 53.

treats of: is concerned with, occupied with or has to do with (a subject); deals with. Page 5.

tricks: special skills or feats (which might cause surprise). Page 160.

trust: to hope or expect confidently. Page viii.

trying: hard to bear or endure; severe, distressing, painful. Page 69.

two-way communication: a two-way cycle of communication. For example: Joe, having originated a communication to Bill and having completed it, may then wait for Bill to originate a communication to Joe, thus completing the remainder of the two-way cycle of communication. Page 115.

unduly: to a very great extent or to an excessive degree. Page 147.

unenlightened: not enlightened. *Enlightened* is to have spiritual or intellectual knowledge or truth; to be free from ignorance, prejudice and superstition. Page 93.

universe: a "whole system of created things." There could be, and are, many universes, and there could be many kinds of universes. These include the MEST universe, that agreed-upon reality of matter, energy, space and time and also our personal universe. Page 5.

unrelenting: not weakening or easing up; without mercy or compassion. Page 126.

unseemly: contrary to accepted standards of good taste or appropriate behavior. Page 116.

unwittingly: unknowingly; unconsciously; without awareness. Page 124.

urges: drives, impulses. Page 37.

valence(s): extra personalities, selves, apparent beingnesses; a false identity assumed unwittingly. Page 87.

vanishes: makes suddenly disappear. Page 89.

vantage point: a position or location that provides a broad view or perspective of something. Page 53.

verbal: consisting of or expressed in words (as opposed to facts or realities). Page 39.

via: by means of. Page 68.

vilify: use abusive language or false and intentionally harmful statements about; speak evil of; swear at. Page 23.

virtues: the ideal qualities in good human conduct. Page 32.

visionaries: dreamers; people whose ideas, plans, etc., are impractical or too fantastic. Page 54.

Voltaire: (1694-1778) French author and philosopher who produced a range of literary works, often attacking injustice and intolerance, and who was imprisoned for writing things that supposedly ridiculed the government. In 1717, while serving a prison term, he finished writing his first play, the success of which made him the greatest French playwright of his time. Page 88.

voluntary: a reference to voluntary muscular reactions, those that are normally controlled by or subject to the individual's conscious choice such as the movement of one's arm. Page 71.

waged: carried on or engaged in. Page 90.

wanting: lacking or absent. Page 53.

war cry: literally a cry or shout of troops in battle. Figuratively it is something shouted to encourage or rally a group; a watchword. Page 57.

warped: turned from the true, natural or right course. Page 79.

wavelength: a wavelength is a characteristic of motion. Many motions are too random, too chaotic to have orderly wavelengths. An orderly wavelength is a flow of motion. It has a regular repeated distance between its crests. Take a rope or the garden hose and give it a flip. You will see a wave travel along it. Energy, whether electrical, light or sound, has some such pattern.

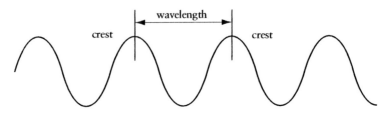

This is a smooth flowing wave. Its length is between crests. It is measured in units of length such as centimeters or inches or feet. Page 66.

weeping: manifesting or giving expression to a strong emotion, usually grief or sorrow, by crying. Page 3.

well: something resembling a *well,* a deep reservoir from which one may draw. Page 2.

Wilhelm, Kaiser: Kaiser Wilhelm II (1859-1941), the last emperor (Kaiser) of Germany who pursued an aggressive program of commercial and colonial expansion and who led Germany into World War I (1914-1918). Page 95.

wise, in this: in this way or in this manner. Page 56.

"world shaker": a person who creates effects of great significance or influence, enough to affect the world. Page 95.

Wundt: Wilhelm Wundt (1832-1920), German psychologist and physiologist; the originator of modern psychology and the false doctrine that Man is no more than an animal. Page 5.

Wundtian: of, like or developed by Wilhelm Wundt (1832-1920). *See also* **Wundt.** Page 6.

yearns: wants something very much, often with a feeling of frustration because of the difficulty or impossibility of fulfilling the desire. Page 55.

yesterday: time in the past, sometimes the recent past. Page 2.

Yoga: a school of Indian religious philosophy advocating and prescribing a course of physical and mental disciplines for attaining liberation from the material world and union of the self with a supreme spirit. Page 113.

$\mathcal{I}$NDEX

A

aberration, 126
    common denominator of, 77
    consideration and, 89
    games and, 139
    mind and, 72

ability
    to be, to do, to have, 32
    to create, 60
    to make a postulate, 60

acknowledgment, 148

action
    automatic, definition, 24
    cycle of, *see* cycle-of-action
    definition, 21
    dictated by reactive mind, 69
    effect in creation, 125

actual
    definition, 22

actual cycle-of-action
    definition, 23
    destruction and, 23
    see also cycle-of-action

affinity, 45–48
    communication and, 48
    definition, 45
    relationship to communication and
        reality, 47

agitation
    loss of havingness and, 164

agreement
    communication and basis for, 48
    communication bridge and, 164
    reality and, 47
    society and, 94

analytical mind
    definition, 68
    somatic mind and, 71

anatomy of control, 78, 79, 150

anchor points
    definition, 73
    space and, 73

anesthetic
    silence in vicinity of person
        under, 70

Anger, 46

animal
    psychology and soulless, 6

Animal Dynamic
    definition, 39

Antagonism, 46

anxiety
    prevention, 114
    survival of identity and, 127

Apathy, 46, 162
    and below, 46

apparency
    definition, 22
    reality and, 24

apparent cycle-of-action, 23
    see also cycle-of-action

Aquinas, Saint Thomas, 5

A-R-C
    definition, 48
    Tone Scale, basis of, 48
    understanding and, 48

A-R-C Triangle, 45–48
    common denominator to all of life's
        activities, 45
    definition, 45

disinterest, 54

distance
affinity and consideration of, 45

doing (doingness), 32
definition, 32, 125
effect and, 125–127

dopiness
loss of havingness and, 154, 164

drills
in Scientology, 6

dwindling spiral, 57

dynamics
concentric circles, series of, 40
conditions-of-existence and, 40
cycle-of-action and, 40
definition, 37
eight, 37–40
Eighth, 39, 40, 76
Fifth, 39
First, 38
Fourth, 38
game condition and, 140
games and, 56
groups, 38
in Dianetics, 39
in Scientology, 39
listed, 38–39
relative importance, 37, 40
Second, 38
Seventh, 39
Sixth, 39
space expanding and, 40
stressing one or a combination
more than others, 37
Third, 38

E

education
in Scientology, 7
not-knowing and, 101
savagery and forbidding, 94
self-created data and, 94

effect
cause and, 89, 95
upset and imbalance of, 91

creation of
attention and, 126
highest purpose in this
universe, 86, 90, 126
despair of creating, 126
doing and, 125–127
effect-point, definition, 91
have and, 127
makes distance, 127
no, see no-effect
responsibility and, 92
security and, 126

effect processes, 125

eight dynamics, see dynamics

Eighth Dynamic, 76
definition, 39
discovering the true, 40

electrical field
body and, 73
definition, 73

electric shock, 74

emotion
affinity and, 46
A-R-C and, 47
energy particles and, 46
tones of, 46

emotional tones, 46

energy
barriers and, 93
definition, 86
emotion and particles of, 46
facsimile and, 72
mental versus physical, 72

Enthusiasm, 46

environment
command of, 88
keep preclear alert to, 160
mental image pictures and, 72
thetan handling, 162

euthanasia, 74
definition, 74

evaluation
Auditor's Code and, 115

evolutionaries
Scientologists and, 1

Exchanged Valence
definition and example, 124

scarcity
of games, 140, 156
science
of life, Scientology and, 96
Science of Survival, 47
Scientologist
Code of a, 116
Scientology, 114
Axioms, 85-86
basic principles of, 15, 26
basics of knowledge and, 90
books and services, 8
definition, 5
dynamics included in, 39
education in, 7
future of, 169
goal of, 107, 151
greatest discovery, 65
how to study, 15
humanities and, vii
intention of, 80
mission of, 1
Preventive, 114
processing, *see* **processing**
psychosomatic ills overcome
and, 114
questions and answers, 5-8
reminding, not teaching, 96
science of life, 96
study of the spirit, 6
use of, 7, 8
codes in, 116, 117
what it can do, 6
what it is, 5-7
Scientology practitioners
validation of, 8
see also **auditor**
Second Dynamic
definition, 38
security, 126
self-created data, 94
Self-determinism, 133-134
game conditions and, 141
games and, 56
goal of Scientology and, 151
Self Dynamic
definition, 38
separateness
freedom and, 160

Separateness (process), 159
Serenity, 46, 141
top of A-R-C Triangle, 47
session
auditor's ability in a, 148
definition, 148
present time problem and, 156
two-way communication and, 162
under auditor's command, 151
Seventh Dynamic
definition, 39
sex
anxieties of, 77
Sex Dynamic
definition, 38
significances, 162
avoid in processing, 162
silence
in vicinity of unconscious
person, 70
Sixth Dynamic
definition, 39
solidity
affinity and, 46
solutions, 141
somatic
process to release, 161
somatic mind, 68, 71-73
description, 71
no "thinkingness," 71
source-point, 91
space
definition, 86
identity and, 124
spirit, 65, 66-67
creator of things, 66
individual is a, 76
Scientology and study of the, 6
separable from the body and
mind, 65
subject of the mind, life and, 26
Spiritual Dynamic
definition, 39
Start-Change-and-Stop, 127, 150-151
anatomy of control, 78
neurosis and psychosis and, 79

239

BE AN EXPERT

IN LIFE ITSELF

Scientology: The Fundamentals of Thought contains the basic principles of Scientology and the most elementary processing.

But to be effective – to be able to apply Scientology with uniformly miracle results – requires training.

How would you like to be instructed by L. Ron Hubbard himself? Well, that's exactly what you can experience. Because, immediately following publication of this book, Ron designed a special course to bring total certainty on these fundamentals – a course he intended for *every* Scientologist.

For each Scientology breakthrough you learn *how* it came to be discovered, the *why* of its effectiveness and the *what* to do in applying them.

All of this in addition to precision exercises and drills to guarantee your certainty of understanding and application – in both *auditing* and *life* – are what awaits you on the Hubbard Qualified Scientologist Course.

A Scientologist is one who can apply Scientology to improve conditions anywhere. Do this course and you'll graduate as a Professional Scientologist – an expert in life itself!

ENROLL TODAY!
Hubbard Qualified Scientologist
C O U R S E

Contact the Registrar at your nearest Church of Scientology
www.scientology.org